Carve Her Name With Pride

The Story of Violette Szabo

R. J. Minney

Pen & Sword
MILITARY

First published in Great Britain in 1956 by George Newnes Ltd.
Reprinted in 1964 by Collins Clear-Type Press and reprinted by Pen &
Sword Military Classics in 2006 & 2008.

This edition published in 2011 in Great Britain by
Pen & Sword Military
an imprint of
Pen & Sword Books Ltd
47 Church Street
Barnsley
South Yorkshire
S70 2AS

ISBN 978-1-84884-742-2

Typeset in 11.5pt Ehrhardt by
Mac Style, Beverley, E. Yorkshire

Printed and bound by CPI Group (UK) Ltd, Croydon, CR0 4YY

Pen & Sword Books Ltd incorporates the Imprints of Pen & Sword
Aviation, Pen & Sword Family History, Pen & Sword Maritime, Pen &
Sword Military, Pen & Sword Discovery, Wharncliffe Local History,
Wharncliffe True Crime, Wharncliffe Transport, Pen & Sword Select, Pen
& Sword Military Classics, Leo Cooper, The Praetorian Press, Remember
When, Seaforth Publishing and Frontline Publishing.

For a complete list of Pen & Sword titles please contact
PEN & SWORD BOOKS LIMITED
47 Church Street, Barnsley, South Yorkshire, S70 2AS, England
E-mail: enquiries@pen-and-sword.co.uk
Website: www.pen-and-sword.co.uk

Contents

"She was the bravest of them all."

ODETTE CHURCHILL

Acknowledgements

I am indebted to a large number of people who helped me unstintingly by giving me their time, their memories of Violette Szabo, letters and photographs, and for going through those sections of the manuscript which dealt with incidents with which they were familiar. Of them all my greatest indebtedness is, of course, to Violette's parents, Mr and Mrs Charles Bushell, with whom I had many talks before they went to Australia, and who have supplemented in long letters every episode on which I sought information. Miss Violet Buckingham, her cousin, Mrs Florence Lucas, aunt, and her son Norman Lucas, Mrs Winifred Sharpe, who was her girlhood friend Winnie Wilson, and Mrs Elsie Grundry, who was with Violette in the ATS, as well as the Battery Commander, Lieutenant-Colonel J.W. Naylor, all helped greatly with the earlier episodes; Colonel Maurice Buckmaster, Miss Vera Atkins, and Mr Selwyn Jepson gave me details of her enlistment, her training and her work as a secret agent, with very valuable supplementations from Robert Maloubier (Robert Mortier), Miss Jacqueline Dufour (Anastasie's sister), Mr Harry Peulevé, and Mr F.F.E. Yeo-Thomas. I owe my thanks also to Monsieur and Madame Renaudie and many farmers and villagers at Salon-la-Tour, to her school teachers, Miss Beatrice Hardy, Miss Margaret Douglas and Miss Elsie Lowlett, to Miss Olive Bird, manageress of the perfumery department at the Bon Marché at Brixton, Sergeant Eric Ford and Miss Eileen R. Smith of the mixed ack-ack battery, Miss

Acknowledgements

Winifred Mason, of the FANYs, Mrs Margaret Edwardes of
Havant, Major Roger de Wesselow, Major Stephen Stewart,
Mr Jerrard Tickell, Mr Paul Dehn, Mr C.M. Gosden, Mr
Bernard Newman, Miss Cynthia Sadler, Miss Jean Overton
Fuller, Miss Peggy Minchin (who was her conducting officer
in Scotland), Mrs Nancy Roberts, Mr Louis Lee-Graham, also
a secret agent, who was a prisoner at Torgau for two years, and
for the Ravensbrück scenes in particular to Mrs Geoffrey
Hallowes (Odette Churchill).

Introduction

This is the story of a girl, born of humble parents, one English, one French, and brought up chiefly in the back streets of London. She did not appear to be different from others. She had no discernible talents. There were no early signs of her being a prodigy either as a pianist or a painter, a singer or a dancer. She had beauty, a haunting beauty, though she did not exploit it. But there were qualities, noticeable only to a few, which, in a moment of crisis and peril, made her resolute, fearless, unresponsive under agonising torture, so that in Britain's proud story she has her place as a heroine.

In the recent war, though millions were engaged in it, individuals had mobility and were able by their ingenuity and valour to win renown. Not many women served as secret agents; the toll was high, for nearly a third of them died. This is the story of one of those who did not come back.

As you read here of her heroic exploits you will no doubt ask yourself: "What were her feelings, what were her thoughts at such moments?" She was more intelligent than many, both boys and girls, who were at school with her. Were her actions then governed by the power of her thoughts, was she able to discipline and control herself by reason? She was imaginative but apparently knew no fear, she was sensitive but not it seems to pain, and her powers of endurance were extraordinary, for she seemed never to run out of strength. Her sense of fun and mischief was not a cover in a moment of tension, for she always had these traits; and her matey-ness was not a war-time development, a drawing together in the face of danger, as happened to so many during the stress of war, even at home, in the shelters.

She was not dominating, assertive, vain or egocentric – extra-ordinarily enough she was not, though so many whose deeds are marked by heroism were. She must have enjoyed, one feels, the notice her beauty attracted, but she did not seem, outwardly at any rate, to be flattered by the attention of men. She seemed to take it as normal and met them on terms of unself-conscious equality, without any coyness or posturing or finesse. But one feels she must have enjoyed the experience of being looked at and admired. By becoming a secret agent she had to reverse this natural instinct, for she had to avoid being conspicuous, nor could her ego be elated by the unusual role she had assumed, for she was unable to talk of it either to her family or her friends, or to proclaim it by any badge or uniform for others to recognise and admire. She had to merge herself into the life around her, especially while moving among the simple country people in enemy-occupied France.

She was indeed simple in herself, devoid of all affectations and completely without guile. But, with the gradual deepening of her purpose beneath her outward airiness and frivolity, she developed instincts of which she had been utterly unaware. Hating domesticity, she cheerfully undertook distasteful chores and eagerly volunteered for work that she knew would be exacting and perilous. She was aware that the price for what she hoped to accomplish might have to be paid with her life; in which event others would, she knew, as readily step in to complete what she had begun. Most of the time she battled alone, and against overwhelming odds, with the cunning and might of the Gestapo and the myriads they employed for their vile tasks. By her daring and astuteness, again and again she managed to outwit them; later the battle assumed even more alarming proportions when she had to turn and fight a powerful detachment of the Das Reich Panzer division, consisting of 400 men and two armoured cars – which roused the admiration even of the enemy. But, thereafter, all the cruel weight of the German nation was used to crush her, but she remained unyielding, although even mature and valiant men have confessed their inability to endure the agony of sustained torture.

Posthumously the George Cross was awarded her. It was presented by King George the Sixth to her daughter, Tania, then a child of four.

Chapter 1

Early Influences

Violette Bushell was the daughter of an English father and a French mother. Her parents met during the First World War while her father, Charles Bushell, was fighting in France. He was billeted at Camiers, just outside Etaples. Mlle Reine Leroy, slight, petite and pretty, was staying in the village too with her cousins. They met, fell in love and after a courtship carried on amid the distractions and dangers of war for two interrupted years, were married just before the Armistice at Pont Rémy, near Abbeville.

Bushell regarded himself as a Cockney, though in fact he was born at Hampstead Norris in Berkshire, where his father was a farmer and a crack shot with a sporting gun. Young Bushell joined the regular army in 1908. He spent some years in the Royal Horse Artillery, transferred to the Royal Flying Corps when it was formed, but his plane crashed and he was invalided out. On the outbreak of war in 1914 he rejoined the army, became a motor driver in the Royal Army Service Corps and was engaged in driving army lorries when he met the girl he was to marry. She, though French by birth, had a partly English ancestry, for she was descended from a Lancashire family named Scott. The war over, the Bushells came to England and their first child, a boy named Roy, was born in London in 1920.

The wave of prosperity which followed the Armistice soon spent itself and daily hundreds of men and women found themselves trudging the streets looking for work. Slowly the great army of unemployed grew. Mr Bushell, having no wish to be one of their number, decided to take his small family to Paris where he felt his energy and enterprise might find an outlet. With his gratuity he bought a large and attractive second-hand car and, using this as a private taxi, he drove visitors not only round Paris, but took them, when required, on much longer journeys. He took, for instance, an American family all the way from Paris to Venice. He had many noteworthy fares, among them the ex-King George of Greece and the much-married American actress Peggy Hopkins Joyce. Mrs Bushell was by now expecting her second child and it was in the British Hospital in Paris that Violette Reine Elizabeth Bushell was born on June 26th, 1921. She was a small baby, scarcely as big as her name. She was dark, strong and very healthy.

Mrs Bushell, taking the child home to their small apartment, looked forward to a life of ease and happiness in Paris, which she knew well, for she had worked there as a midinette and later as a dressmaker for Lucille and Paul Poiret. But they did not stay as long as she would have liked. In less than three years they were back in England. Times were not so good in Paris, and anyway Mr Bushell was glad to be out of it, for he could not cope with the language despite all his years in France during and since the war.

But with nothing definite to come to in England it was to his parents' home at Hampstead Norris that he took his family, Violette aged three by now, and the boy just over four. Once again his resourcefulness supplied Mr Bushell with an income at a time when unemployment was soaring to terrifying heights. He started a private bus service. He drove the bus himself and picked up passengers whenever hailed as he plied to and fro between Hampstead Norris and Newbury.

So Violette's earliest memories were almost entirely of the English countryside. Of Paris she retained fleeting sounds and scenes which were to reverberate as echoes when she revisited it many years later at a time of tension, for, at such times more than at any other, nostalgic memories are apt to possess one and to offer a certain melancholy solace. At Hampstead Norris she played in the garden, roved the fields, fearless of cows, bulls or even mice, as children generally are, but she was to retain this fearlessness. Papa used to place an apple on her head to Mama's recurrent alarm while he tried his prowess with a gun in the familiar William Tell manner. Fortunately he never failed, but the child did not flinch once. Nor, when, after persistent effort, she climbed by herself a lofty wall and began to walk along the top of it, did she cry when she fell off. Her head was cut open, her nose broken, but there were no tears. It was Mama who cried and fussed and carried her, a mutilated and bleeding little mite, up to her bed and even Papa was a little pale with fright. But Violette merely smiled at them from her bed and reassured them by saying: "It doesn't hurt much – not really" – and they were to learn with the passing years that nothing ever did. She shut her eyes, said she wanted to 'go dodo' and fell asleep at once.

She was a sturdy little child, strong and always active. Nothing her elder brother attempted seemed beyond her, and she would challenge him to fresh feats of prowess which, when he failed, she would undertake herself and accomplish successfully to the astonishment of all and to his intense annoyance. "She should have been a boy," both her father and mother declared, for she was not at all interested in dolls and other girlish diversions of the sedentary kind, which is perhaps not surprising seeing that her sole companion was a boy. But they noticed also a boyish impish-ness, an unflagging indulgence in mischief, which earned her inevitably the tag of 'little monkey'. This apparently she never outgrew, for even in maturity this faculty for fun was undimmed. But in childhood, as later, her pranks rarely got her into a scrape: occasionally the blame was visited on another, as, for example, when she induced her father to lift her by her ankles high above his head and waltz her round the room with her head imperilled by central ceiling lights and the hard, unyielding edges of ward-robe tops and brackets. Not that she feared or evaded punishment. Those who knew her as a child remember quite vividly the way she would look right into one's eyes and say: "Yes, I did it." Nothing seemed to daunt her. She shinned up trees, making her brother Roy follow her until she got him so high that he was too scared to attempt coming down without help.

3

He called shrilly for Dad or anyone else who could hear and with assistance was brought down again. Violette could hardly be blamed, for she had gone a great deal higher and needed no assistance at all to descend. She turned cartwheels all over the house, in the sitting-room, the kitchen, in and out of bedrooms. She was like a fire-cracker. She jumped into the river, any river, and taught herself to swim and was soon a great deal better at it than her brother.

Life in the country did not last long. The family moved to London where Papa felt he could make a better living by buying and selling motor-cars. Mama was by now expecting her third child. It was a boy this time and was named John.

Living in the close, confined, often stifling back streets of Fulham, Violette missed the freedom and freshness of the countryside, as Mama missed them too, for much of her life had been spent in the countryside in France. So she took Vi, as the child was now inevitably called, on visits to an uncle and aunt and a host of cousins of Mr Bushell's, who lived in Twickenham. Violet Buckingham, the only girl in this family, though some years older than Violette (who was given her name in its French form), remembers these visits well and in particular the first time the child stayed with her for a period of three weeks. Violette was not quite five, "but she played me up quite a bit. Once, when we were out for a walk, she ran off all by herself, in and out of various roads, with me panting behind until she was right out of sight. I was terrified that she would rush into the traffic on the main road. I called after her but got no answer and eventually, after an agony of anxiety, I found the little monkey some distance away, standing with her two arms round a red pillar box, smiling impishly at me, vastly amused at the flurry and concern she had caused.

"She had an adventurous spirit," says Violet Buckingham, "and thought running away was great fun. She was constantly doing it. She used to run remarkably well – I found it impossible to keep up with her. If she was missing for a moment I never knew what mischief she was up to or what danger she was in, either on land or in the water, for she was constantly drifting off towards the river.

C.N.P   B

4

"She was really afraid of nothing. I remember one day she was upstairs helping me to make the beds – or rather trying hard to. We were busy for a while, then I missed her and to my horror saw her seated on the window-sill with her legs dangling out. She was talking cheerfully to my youngest brother, who had just got back from school. When I told her to get in she refused and was about to drop on to the scullery roof below, walk along its ledge and leap down to join my brother, but I stopped her just in time and brought her back in tears into the room. I had to console her by letting her make my brother's bed into an apple-pie disorder. All my five brothers were very fond of her. They used to throw her up into the air and toss her from one to another like a ball. She thought it great fun. She used to spar quite a lot with them and went at it hammer and tongs with the youngest one who, though some years older, was nearer her own size. At skipping she beat them all. She loved getting on to the back of the motor-bike. Speed, thrill, excitement – that's what she loved. She had a temper too and a very strong will. You could never make her do anything she didn't want to. She would purse her lips together and her little chin would harden as she said – I can hear her saying it now – 'I won't. I *won't.*' She said it with emphasis and determination. She had great determination – even when she grew up."

She seems to have got her determination and her resourcefulness from her father – and also her gaiety, for Mama was a quiet little woman, very charming and quite placid, taking all the knocks of life without turning a hair.

Towards the end of 1926, when Violette was five-and-a-half, Mrs Bushell had her fourth child, a boy again whom she called Noel. It was the year of the General Strike. Unemployment rose by leaps and bounds and things weren't going too well again for Mr Bushell. So the entire family went to try their luck in France. They lived this time with Mrs Bushell's relatives at Pont Rémy. This had been the scene of their marriage. There was a stir of happier memories and their hopes ran high, for expenses were negligible in the house they shared with her father and his sister, Tante Maria. Her own sister, the children's Aunt Marguerite, kept house for them. Pont Rémy is a small town with four bridges across the River Somme. Open country lies all round and not far away is the main road from Boulogne to Paris. Mr Bushell found conditions not much better here. Yet they stayed for three years. Mrs Bushell made a bit of money by dressmaking, while her husband tried his hand at this and that. But the children were growing fast and it was felt that there should be an end to this nomadic life. They decided to return to England so that Violette and the three boys might have the benefit of an English education. Violette was nearly nine now. She had received some schooling at the local convent and spoke French fluently – they all did, except Papa who still found the language quite beyond him.

In England, they roved for a further three years, going first to West Kensington, then all the way to Leicester, then back again to London to live in Bayswater. The children moved from school to school. Violette had to face the ordeal of receiving instruction in a language with which she was only colloquially familiar. She seemed an alien to the other girls, for she spoke with a marked accent. But her voice was as pretty as her face and they found it fascinating to listen to her as, with her large violet eyes wide open, she told of the fun and diversity that life offered to a little girl in France.

Papa was out almost all the time looking for a job and with Mama away most of the day, for she provided much of the income now and had to go out fitting her customers, the care of the boys fell inevitably to Violette. She had to wash and dress them and prepare a snack of sorts when she and Roy and John came back from school for their midday dinner; little Noel, not quite three, needed of course additional attention. These were among the things she did not enjoy doing, but as the only girl in the family, it was a role she had to assume. She undertook it cheerfully, for she never grumbled or sulked – that formed no part of her temperament. It helped, of course, to develop in her a sense of responsibility, of keeping to a routine, since meals had to be served at well-defined times and they had to be back in school before the bell went. But they all looked extremely clean and neat in the clothes their mother made for them and they had remarkably fine manners.

In the summer of 1932 the family went to live in Brixton where they were to remain for the rest of Violette's life. She had already, at eleven, run through nearly half her allotted span. Hitler even now stood snarling in the wings, getting ready – for the grim drama in which she was to play so heroic a role.

Chapter 2

Brixton

When Mr Bushell went looking for rooms in Brixton he said, aware that landladies may jib at a large family, that he had three sons, one of whom was going to stay with relatives in France.

Mrs Tripp, who let out rooms at No. 12 Stockwell Park Walk, showed him the small top flat and the family moved in two weeks later. It was then discovered that there was also a little girl. The two boys who came were Roy and John. The youngest, Noel, had been parked with Aunt Marguerite at Pont Rémy.

Mrs Tripp, a quaint soul with a most generous heart, mothered the enormous household of assorted lodgers. She had with her her own two children, now almost grown up, and a nephew and niece, both orphans, whom she had taken under her care from childhood. Of these the one nearest in age to Violette was Winnie Wilson, five years her senior and at that stage not regarded as a contemporary, for there is little that a girl of sixteen can have in common with a girl of only eleven. Among the lodgers was a German named von Kettler: he was always referred to as 'Mr Hitler', casually at first with that name so much even then in the newspapers, but constantly after the remarkable rise to power a few months later of the Charlie Chaplin-like corporal who became the Führer. How Kettler got the 'von' nobody knows; it is possible that he did not assume it since his father was a friend of von Papen's, then actually the German Chancellor and at one time a German spy. But the link was without significance, for von Kettler has no part in this story other than by his presence in the household, where he remained until the time of Munich and showed a desperate anxiety amid the flurry and excitement to return to his own home so as not to be seized and interned here in the event of a war. He was regarded by the others as very charming and was always smartly dressed in a household that was far from affluent. But Violette saw little of him for she did not mix much with the grown-ups downstairs. Her father, on the other hand, was constantly with them, playing billiards with the boys, swopping yarns, going round for a drink at the pub, gay, genial and known to all as Charlie.

The first they saw of Violette was one evening when a timid knock was heard at the kitchen door and a dark attractive little girl came in holding out some coppers in her hand. She wanted a sixpence for the gas-meter.

Winnie, who was sitting at the kitchen table working at her shorthand, remembers the moment well. "The little girl was very beautiful. Both my aunt and I gasped when we saw her and Aunt said afterwards, 'What a lovely little girl – isn't she remarkably pretty?'

"She had large violet eyes with a dash of green in them. They were very expressive eyes and seemed to change in colour. She had very long black silken lashes and two tiny beauty spots, one by the side of her mouth, the other on her chin.

"She had a small but fascinating voice. There was a marked French accent, which she later lost, but at that time one might almost say she spoke broken English. At any rate that is the impression we had. She was quite unaffected – a very natural, unspoilt child. We all got to like her very much. Aunt was particularly fond of her."

Violette and the two boys went to the school in Stockwell Road, just round the corner. It is an enormous London County Council school and takes nearly 1,000 children, boys as well as girls, about a third of them juniors. The building is unattractive and stands back from the busy Stockwell Road with its roar of traffic, its buses, its many cycle shops and second-hand car marts, all painted a hideous red, its ill-kempt housewives with their shopping bags and baskets, its boxes of fruit and vegetables spilling from the shops on to the pavement, its stalls of whelks and winkles and, at that time, the buzz, flash and clatter too of large bouncing trams. Violette and her brothers had to cross the road to school, with its apron of a playground in front, its large solitary tree and high walls topped by wire netting.

Quite a large number of the children here were the children of the costermongers who sold flowers and fruit from barrows in Brixton Market. A few were the children of theatrical parents, of whom there had once been many in this neighbourhood; but their numbers had been declining for some time and were swelled only at intervals by troupes of children who performed in the evenings in pantomimes or as a dance act on the music-hall stage and were of course required by law to attend a school. A small sprinkling of the children came from the homes of policemen, of whom quite a number lived in the district and there are now even more. Surprisingly they all mixed well, if a little noisily and boisterously.

But even in this varied setting Violette stood out, partly because of her French accent and exotic mannerisms and gestures, but chiefly because she was strong-limbed, lithe and exceedingly daring. There was no drain-pipe she could not climb, no wall she could not scale, feats that were often beyond the scope of even the boys; when faced with a challenge and pitted specifically against another, to the shouted delight of them all, Violette always triumphed. It was a skill she had acquired in her endless contests against her brothers in the countryside and in the water, in England and in France, and even inside the home, for Mrs Tripp and the others found the Bushell children involved in an unceasing clatter overhead and could never determine whether the girl was fighting both her brothers at once or was merely having a game that involved a great deal of rough-and-tumble.

It is denied, even by her schoolmistress, that there was any sense of superiority or boastfulness in Violette's behaviour. She did it all confidently and quite unself-consciously, and, far from rousing jealousies and antagonism, she managed to win the admiration as well as the affection of those with whom she talked and played. "Her manner was friendly, her disposition gay and vivacious, and with those large, lovely eyes, she looked like something not quite of this world," says one of her teachers. "Indeed with her ability to speak French and her life in the French countryside of which she often talked, she seemed to many of the children to possess the key to two worlds – and yet she remained quite modest and unassuming, as though it was natural for her to be different."

The teachers found she had a quick and lively mind. Although she had already been to a number of English schools, there was still a need for much adjustment, not only in arithmetical calculations, which in her early instruction had revolved wholly round the metric system, but in the use of phrases and idioms which differed so markedly from those current in her home where she still talked a great deal of French with her mother and brothers.

"Physically she was very strong," says the physical training instructress, "she had firm and sturdy limbs and was quite outstanding in everything I set the girls to do." But at history and geography she was not quite so good, however hard she strove in those overcrowded gas-lit classrooms. At needlework, as at all other domestic tasks, such as cooking and work in the laundry, which she really detested, her progress was equally lagging.

"She vibrated with personality. She seemed to have a lot of push and drive. She was a sort of immature leader," says the then headmistress; "where she led the others followed eagerly – and the interesting thing is that she did not lead them into any mischief or naughtiness. She was indeed very amenable to discipline. Mind you, she had a strong will, but it was well controlled."

She apparently never got into trouble. It is of course possible that she contrived to be careful enough never to be caught at her innocent mischief. If indeed she possessed such early astuteness it would certainly have been a great asset to her in the work she was called upon to undertake during the war; but this is doubtful. The one thing above all else that they recall in school as at home is that she would never tell a lie. She faced up to every situation unflinchingly and at times a little defiantly.

It was before the days of school meals. The really necessitous children were collected by bus and taken off to an LCC centre where special meals were served to them. The others either ate sandwiches their mothers had packed for them or went home for their midday dinner. Violette and her brothers went home. They would not want the stigma of poverty to be applied to them, for they were proud, and besides Papa was working now for a builder he had met through the Tripps and was indeed fortunate to get a job so soon after the 1931 crisis when unemployment spread even more rapidly than before. Through good times and bad Violette and her brothers always looked well cared for and well fed. In school she wore the navy tunic and red jersey which the children wear to this day.

Going home they sometimes encountered in the street some of the rougher boys who, having finished their meal of fish and chips out of a newspaper, lay in wait to rub the greasy wrapping into the face of any passing girl. They did not, however, try this on Violette, for they must have known that, although she was always ready to join in every sort of fun, one could only go so far with her and that, when roused, she would turn and fight them with her fists, whether her brothers helped her or not. So she was allowed always to pass unmolested. In contrast to this readiness to fight like a fiend if anyone tried to get the better of her, she was generosity itself at all other times and gave away her most prized possessions if her brothers and even casual school acquaintances coveted them. But if one tried to take anything from her by force or by stealth, it generally ended in a stand-up fight and she was almost always victorious. As a result she was able to cow them with just a glare of anger and defiance. They knew that nothing would make her give way by one iota. One would not have thought, looking at this pretty wide-eyed girl of eleven or so, that she had so much determination and inflexibility in her.

The school holidays led to the children being divided up. Some went to stay with Mr Bushell's sister, who had a pub in Hereford: in the summer, Violette and one or other of the boys generally went to France to spend a few weeks with Aunt Marguerite.

Stockwell Park Walk, the street in which they lived, was a turning off the main road, not many yards from the school. It was a small street which had known better days, but now had just a few unpretentious houses. It ran down to what was once The Green, but the Astoria Cinema stood there now and the queues, when the film was popular, wound round to the back and extended almost to their front door. At night, as she lay in bed in the curtained landing that was her bedroom, Violette could hear the whoops of cowboys and Indians, the firing of pistol shots, the whang of an arrow, and of course the gay syncopation of the music on the sound track of each picture.

They lived here for three years. Noel came back from France and the flat became more crowded than ever with six in it; but Roy, leaving school, got a job as a page boy at the Savoy Hotel, where his mother often went to attend to her customers, and things became a little easier financially. Soon Mrs Bushell was expecting her fifth child and it became obvious that they would have to find a much larger place for Mr Bushell's mother had also come by now to live with them. They did not need to go far. A hundred yards or so down Stockwell Road, another turning on the same side is Burnley Road. There at No. 18 they found ampler accommodation in the basement and ground floor, with a room on the first floor and the use of a small garden at the back; and here the next month still another boy was born called Richard. He was of course largely under Violette's care while her mother was at work. She attended to him at the midday interval from school and again in the afternoon when she got home. For the rest of the time the child was left with Mrs Tripp in Stockwell Park Walk.

Theirs was one of the smaller houses in Burnley Road. Winter and summer children played in the street with a ball and tore along on skates, while the smaller girls sat on the kerb and nursed their shabby cloth dolls. Violette would have joined the boys undoubtedly in their sturdier games, and possibly did when her father wasn't about, for he sternly forbade any playing in the street.

In June 1935, Violette, having reached the age of fourteen, insisted on leaving school. Nothing would induce her to stay on, much though her parents wanted her to. It was her mother's hope that she too might be a dressmaker. There was a ready income from it as they all knew, for it had sustained them through many difficult years. But try how she would, Mrs Bushell could not get Violette sufficiently interested in using her needle, except for emergency repairs. Violette's own great ambition was to be a hairdresser, to work in a shop and one day perhaps to have a place of her own, where women would come and have their hair washed and curled in new styles of her devising. Her parents, recognising it as a humdrum occupation for one bubbling over with so much personality, at last, after much persistent persuasion, agreed to let her have her own way. But various sums ranging from £50 to £100 were demanded as a premium for her training and this they were quite unable to raise. So Violette had to adjust her aspirations and be content with a job in a shop. A place was found for her with a French corsetiere in South Kensington. She had to get there very early in the morning, clean out the place, make coffee in the forenoon and tea in the afternoon for the other girls, and go out delivering parcels all day long. She found it boring in the extreme, but revelled in her new-found liberty.

At weekends and during the long summer evenings she diverted herself, as always, out of doors. She joined a cycling club and soon became so skilled that the others were no longer a match for her. Wearing shorts, even in midwinter, with her bare knees flashing up and down, she used to tear away in front of the rest on their Sunday morning outings and often would turn off to visit her cousin Violet Buckingham, who had suffered so many fluttering anxieties when Violette was left in her charge as a child. Miss Buckingham now lived at Harmondsworth on the Great West Road. Having arrived there, Violette never stayed long. After performing many acrobatic twists and turns on her bicycle she would set off with the five Buckingham boys for Burnham Beeches or for Runnymede, where she would plunge into the river and indulge in all forms of aquatic tomfoolery. They generally

14

finished up at a pub where she loved to play darts and in time became good at that too.

At times one or more of her brothers came with her and they made a party of eight or ten, with her as the only girl among so many cousins and brothers. If the weather was wet or cold, instead of going into the country, the boys would induce her to come into London and they would go to one of the shooting galleries which at that time abounded in the West End; and at the gallery at Marble Arch or in Coventry Street or the Strand each would try to match the other's skill at winning a prize, which was generally no more than a packet of cigarettes. The boys were good at this but she had no intention of being outclassed. With her great determination and the aid of a steady hand and eye, she was able to forge ahead of them and was eventually refused a gun because she unfailingly won all the prizes.

She liked being with men. She liked the terms of easy equality, the chaffing and chipping that went on. She liked the opportunity it offered for emulation and was spurred on to greater endeavours, to see if she could not meet them on their own ground and do even better – and generally she did. She was emerging from childhood, and these were the lines along which she developed.

She very rarely settled down with a book. She was not fond of reading, but occasionally she would be seen curled up in a chair at home, her head bent as she pored over a magazine or a book that happened to engross her, and, seeking what it was, again and again her parents were puzzled by her choice, for it was not girls' stories that she read, not romances or even books and articles on sport, but stories about spies. Generally they were women spies. She read two or three books on Mata Hari and used to go round to the public library to ask for more. They wondered at the flights of fancy of this child of fourteen. Was this the sort of role in which she fancied herself with her recurrent daring and her innocent devilry? Did she, while cleaning out the shop in South Kensington and going out on her varied errands, or when changing her little brother's nappies and giving him his bottle, dream of venturing into the midst of some imagined enemy, vamping some exalted statesman with her beautiful eyes and hiding important documents in her corsage? Of course it was all nonsense and they put it down to her childish love of excitement.

She certainly caused them a great deal of excitement and anxiety some months later when she failed to return home after a long day at work. Mrs Bushell couldn't imagine where she had got to. Had she gone on to see the Buckinghams? Was she swimming in the river at Runnymede or had she gone to one of the near-by baths at Clapham or Camberwell? Perhaps she was at a shooting gallery or had gone to the pictures with one of the other girls at the shop? Surely she would have told them she was going to be late, got a message through somehow even if no one was at home. Mrs Bushell phoned the shop, but there was of course no one there at that hour, so she could do nothing but wait. Mr Bushell, however, intended to deal sternly with Violette when she got back.

The evening advanced and there was still no sign of her. Mrs Bushell, not unnaturally, got increasingly alarmed. Had the child met with an accident? Had she been drowned? Then, her normal calm asserting itself, she wondered if Violette had gone to bed with a headache. She hurried upstairs to the little room on the first floor, but the bed was empty. Her alarm grew as she saw that the dressing-gown, the nightdress, the slippers and all the toilet fittings on the dressing-table were missing. It was obvious now that Violette had packed her things and left. She knew that Violette disliked the drab monotony of the daily round at the corset shop and with certain chores at home on top of it things had no doubt completely got her down.

But where could she have gone? In a panic Mrs Bushell rushed round to see some of Violette's friends, girls who had been at school with her and lived not far away. But none of them knew of her whereabouts. It was now getting on for midnight and the alarm of the family may be imagined if one remembers that Violette was not much more than fourteen.

The Bushells decided that it might be best after all if they got in touch with the police. They went round to the station and reported that their daughter was missing, dreading all the time that the police might already have bad news to impart. But fortunately they had none. Taking down particulars of her dress and appearance, the police asked:

"Has she any relatives she may have gone to?"

"Most of her relatives are in France," said Mrs Bushell.

"She could have gone there, of course."

"Oh no," said Mrs Bushell, "she was there only a few weeks ago."

"Has she her own passport?" the police asked.

"Yes," said Mrs Bushell. "She has her own passport."

"Do you know," they inquired, "if her passport's at home?"

"I didn't look," said Mrs Bushell, "I'll go home and see." Hurrying back she discovered that the passport was not there. The police were instantly informed and she supplied at the same time the address of Aunt Marguerite at Pont Rémy.

The police took up this trail. Inquiries made in France showed that Violette had been seen in Pont Rémy. They tried to contact Mlle Marguerite Leroy, but learned that she was no longer there. She had left a few days before for Valenciennes.

Violette, faced on arrival with this dilemma, was neither bewildered nor baffled. A resourceful child for her years, she soon surmounted her difficulties.

"Nothing ever defeated Violette," Mrs Bushell says; but she was worried all the same when another day passed without Violette being found. The child had meanwhile, although by now almost penniless, managed to locate her aunt's whereabouts and had gone on to Valenciennes where she eventually traced the friends with whom Aunt Marguerite was staying. This, in due course, was reported by the French police to the police at Brixton, and the Bushell family sighed at last with relief. But Mr Bushell was very angry.

When Violette returned she had to find a new job and jobs weren't at all easy to find at that time. Eventually she got into Woolworth's in Oxford Street where she served at the counter as a sales girl. 'Nothing Over Sixpence' was the slogan at the time, and the alleys were thronged with shoppers, particularly at the lunch-hour. Her father too was fortunate enough to fall on his feet now with an excellent job at Rotax, the firm which made electrical equipment for aircraft.

Violette, who always had a great love for music and was often as a child found humming a little tune she had heard, sung possibly by a strolling player in the street, made an effort to improve her musical education. She took lessons on the violin, but made little progress. She thought the piano might be easier and turned to that, but it was a slow and painful process, so she contented herself by going to dances where she could express herself with her limbs. Her progress at this was rapid, for she gave a lot of time to it, going to dances with her brother Roy or with one of the Buckingham boys. In a little while there wasn't a dance she could not do. She evolved steps of her own and people drew back on the dance floor to watch as she whirled past gaily. As a variant to these outings she stayed at home and joined the small card-party Mama often had in the evenings. It was usually pontoon, but Violette never had any luck at it. "She was a good loser though," says Mama, "which was just as well because she always lost."

Her cousin Violet Buckingham, who saw much of her at this stage of adolescent development, mentions that, despite her athleticism and her love for dancing, which was often almost acrobatic, she somehow escaped being either noisy, raucous or crude. She had indeed a grace and a gentleness which were quite unexpected, and very marked feminine traits, such as her love for fine clothes. In that strange amalgam within her there was a great capacity for sympathy and a tenderness which constantly showed itself, and she was able to remain perfectly calm and self-possessed when others were flurried and distracted. For example, after saving for some months for it, Violette bought herself a new bicycle of which she was very proud. She rode it all the way to Harmondsworth to show it to her cousin and was eager that she should try it out. Violet Buckingham got on, swooped delightedly along the road and on her return, while trying to negotiate her way through the narrow gate, she fell and lay sprawled along the newly gravelled drive, her knees terribly bruised and bleeding. "I felt awfully ill," says Miss Buckingham, "and could hardly move. My mother rushed out, but – and this is what surprised us – it was Violette who took complete charge of the situation. She raised me up and took me into the house. There she bathed my knees and bandaged them, then made me a strong cup of tea. About three weeks later, while we were in the garden, Violette saw a stray cat go by, limping. Picking it up, she saw that one of its paws was hurt. She instantly bathed the injured paw, brought the cat some warm milk and generally made a fuss of it. The cat would not leave after that and remained with us for the rest of its life."

It was a happy girlhood, though in view of the conditions prevailing at the time often an uncertain one. She had to take the job that was going and when retrenchment imposed a reduction in the staff she had to try to find another of a somewhat similar kind. Many thousands of girls of her age went through the same uncertainties in those years of depression and had to do without diversions and often even without necessities. But Violette kept cheerful and had fun. Her sense of mischief, given an outlet from her earliest childhood, exercised itself harmlessly in making apple-pie beds for her brothers, sprinkling itching powder in the beds of the Buckingham boys and using quite divertingly some of the things one buys at small cost for the perpetration of practical jokes, such things as a rubber mat attached to a tube which tilted your plate when you sat down to eat. They were rather childish and were not always received with laughter. Often her brothers got furious, but her air of 'do your damnedest' made them realise that it was not the slightest use for them to be physically menacing. It was better indeed to accept the joke – and they did.

In the autumn of 1937, shortly after she was sixteen, Violette went to her first ball. Her brother Roy, who was still working at the Savoy Hotel, was invited to the staff dance and he took his sister as his partner. It was a great moment for her. The whole family shared in the excitement. Mrs Bushell made her a lovely evening frock, the first long dress Violette had ever worn. It was of white satin trimmed with gold lamé. There were little gold slippers to go with it and the landlady's daughter, who lived in the flat above, gave her a gold snake necklace to wear for the occasion. All agreed that Violette looked lovely as she set out, and at the dance too she attracted a great deal of attention.

She was blossoming now into lovely young womanhood and wherever she went boys inevitably turned to look at her. In the streets they whistled after her, but she walked on unheeding. At parties the men swarmed round her. She was told incessantly that she ought to be a film star. Finding herself without work for a time, she went along to a film studio and took a job as an extra. But no director singled her out from the crowd. No offer was made to train her as an actress and, being without the means to pursue it herself, she reverted to the humdrum role of a shop girl.

But of her pretty frock she made the utmost use. With Roy or one of her cousins, John or Charles Buckingham, or Norman Lucas, Aunt Florence's son, if he happened to be up in town, she went to dance after dance and many were the rows she had with Papa if she happened to stay out after eleven at night. He refused to recognise that at sixteen one was grown up. Mama declined to take sides, but says: "She was so proud of her lovely evening gown, I could not blame her for wanting to show it off."

Without fail every year she still went to France for a few weeks in the summer. She was in fact with her Aunt Marguerite at Pont Rémy, near Abbeville, when Hitler attacked Poland on September 1st, 1939. France by virtue of her treaty was immediately drawn into the war. The holiday had, of course, to be cut short. With Violette was her youngest brother Dickie, aged only four. They had the utmost difficulty in getting a boat back, but managed, with Aunt Marguerite raising her voice amid the chaos and confusion at Calais, to get on to one that was just leaving and they arrived in England only a few hours before England too was at war.

Chapter 3

The War Breaks Out

Violette was eighteen when the war broke out. Soon after her return from France, she got a job as a sales girl in the perfumery department of that popular store the Bon Marché at Brixton. It was right in the heart of the setting with which she had been familiar through childhood, girlhood and what she now regarded as being grown up.

It did not apparently occur to her at this stage to do any war work, though all three services were recruiting girls of her age – the ATS, the WAAF and the WRENS; nor did she think of going into a munitions factory or of work on the land. Not that the war had not been brought close to her. She was in France during the stir and uneasiness of the call-up, which affected all the men at Pont Rémy and at Abbeville. At home her brother Roy joined up at once. He went into the Royal Army Medical Corps. Her father, not young or fit enough for military service, was working in an aircraft factory at Morden in Surrey. John, the brother next below her in age, was only fifteen, but he too joined up before long and went into REME. The two youngest boys, Noel, aged thirteen, and Dickie, only four, were evacuated to live with relatives in the country. Mama, being French, was very worked up and could think of nothing but the war, which had involved France twice in her own lifetime.

But Violette stayed on at the Bon Marché during that first quiet winter of the war. Despite the black-out and the rationing, and the Buckingham boys and her cousin Norman Lucas as well as two of her brothers being involved in it, the war somehow seemed remote to her. One saw, of course, many uniforms in the streets and the sky was full of those amiable silver monsters the barrage balloons, but life still went on more or less normally. One could go to the flicks or go out dancing in the evening. She did. The idea that there was something she could and should do in the war germinated extremely slowly in her mind.

She was greeted by many on her short walk from her home in Burnley Road to the Bon Marché and exchanged passing jests with them. At the shop they found her self-assured and efficient. Her accurate and attractive pronunciation of the names of the French perfumes greatly impressed the customers. There was still, happily, quite a large range of choice, both of perfumes and cosmetics, and as Christmas approached the display was widened to include fancy goods and gifts. Customers poured in all day long and Violette and the dozen or so other girls were kept extremely busy.

"She certainly had a way with her," says Miss Olive Bird, who was, as she still is, the manageress of the department. "Her pleasant, half playful manner went down well with the customers. She was a very good worker. The other girls liked her enormously, as I did too. She was really a delightful person to be with – always happy, always laughing."

The simple dress she was required to wear suited her slight, slim figure. Her dark hair, her sallow complexion and her large sparkling eyes made everyone turn to look again and come up, eager to be served by her.

She stayed until April. Then the war really got going. Denmark and Norway had been invaded by the Germans and the stir of events made her aware that she should do much more than serve in a shop. She had been seeing something of Winnie Wilson, the girl who lived downstairs when the Bushells were in Stockwell Park Walk. Though older than Violette, the difference in their years no longer mattered now that Violette was grown up. With their homes so close together, they often stopped and talked in the street and spent an occasional evening at the pictures or in a dance hall.

Discussing the war with her, Violette announced that she had decided to leave the shop. She could not stay on now, she said.

Winnie Wilson, who is now Mrs Sharpe, says: "Violette kept saying to me she'd like to do some war work. As I had had a nervous breakdown not long before, I told her: 'Don't join one of the services. I'd like to come with you and I can't do anything strenuous. What about the Land Army?'

"Vi said 'All right'. So we went together to Tothill Street in Victoria and were sent to pick strawberries at Fareham in Hampshire."

Fareham, a small market town, stands on a creek known as The Lake, which dips down to Portsmouth Harbour. All round is fruit-growing country. The girls slept in tents, about ten or twelve to a tent. There were quite a number of girls, and a small band of gipsies who lived nearby in their caravans. On a cliff just above a small pebbled beach was a solitary searchlight battery manned by a group of marines in khaki.

Violette had here her first experience of an air raid, for London had not yet been bombed and the Battle of Britain was only just about to begin.

"When the raid began," says Winnie, "the woman warden insisted that we should all go to the shelters, but nothing would budge Vi. She refused point blank to come. Everybody else went, but Vi stayed in the tent.

"Bombs were dropped and one of them hit an oil storage depot not far away. Soon the air was filled with the acrid smell of burning oil. Our warden, thinking it might be a gas attack, made us put on our gas-masks. She got worried about Vi lying there in the tent with no protection of any kind, so she went along, with her gas-mask on, to fetch her.

"She found Vi fast asleep. She shook her and shook her and finally woke her up. Vi, seeing a gas-mask so close to her face, couldn't imagine what on earth was going on. She said afterwards that it gave her quite a fright, but I don't believe it did, for she turned over and went to sleep again. Vi used to say: 'You've got to take a chance in life. All life is a chance really.' That's the way she looked at things always. She was utterly fearless."

After their day's work in the fields, Violette and Winnie and at times one or two of the others, changing from their rough dungarees to something more comfortable, would go down to the pebbled beach and lie there, jesting and talking through the long rainless summer evenings of that remarkable June of 1940. At times they sang choruses and they were joined quite often by some of the boys from the searchlight battery on the cliff who brought down a portable gramophone to which they tried to dance, but it was not at all easy on pebbles. The boys had cigarettes and chocolates which they distributed most generously and the girls in return gave them jugs full of strawberries which formed their share of the day's pickings. Occasionally they were invited by the boys to the camp and danced there in more comfort; or they went along together, a group of ten or more of them, to the nearby pub, where they played darts and drank beer. Often at night they could hear the anti-aircraft guns at Portsmouth and at Hayling Island firing at intruding enemy aircraft.

One evening, while Winnie and Violette were out for a walk on their own, they came across some of the gipsies. Winnie says one of the men, who was a little tipsy, came up to her and slipped his arm round her waist. "Come along," he said, his grip tightening. "Come along and have a drink with us."

"I was terrified. I struggled, but he would not let go. Vi was some distance behind me, but, hearing me cry out and seeing me struggling, she rushed up and, with her hands on her hips, faced the gipsy defiantly. 'Leave her alone,' she said in a sharp voice, 'or I'll let you have it.'

"I thought the others who were looking on – there were about five or six of them – would laugh at a little chit of a girl challenging a group of gipsies. But they didn't. They didn't even intervene.

"Vi really looked wonderful – pretty, but stern and quite unafraid, despite the odds against us. The man glared at her for a moment, then released his hold of me and, rejoining the others in his party, walked on with them. I thought it was amazingly plucky of Vi to do that. I was too terrified to speak or even walk. But she comforted me and helped me back to our camp."

While they were at Fareham, France fell and the war took on a much grimmer aspect. The assault on Britain by air began and the Battle of Britain was fought out overhead at intervals all day long. This made Violette conscious that such contribution as she was making to the war effort by working on the land was relatively quite negligible. She wanted to do much more and talked to Winnie of going back and joining the ATS or one of the other services open to women, even though Winnie, as she realised, would not be able to accompany her.

They returned to town. She found her mother, normally so calm and placid, most gravely concerned about what was happening in France. There had been fighting at Abbeville and all round her own home. Dunkirk followed, with further evacuations from Le Havre and St Valery: and then came the shaming surrender by Pétain who was now trying, with Laval, to run the country from Vichy at the dictate of the Germans.

Violette had been home only a day or so when her mother said: "Tomorrow is Bastille Day – our *Quatorze Juillet*. There are a lot of French soldiers in London, heartbroken at what has been happening to our country. It will be a sad anniversary for them so far away from home. They will be feeling lost and lonely. Why don't you, Vi darling, go out tomorrow and bring one of them back to spend the evening here with us. It will at least be of some comfort for him to be with French people. Don't you think so?"

Violette thought it a good idea. But she was diffident about going alone on so delicate a quest. So she slipped along to her friend Winnie Wilson and they arranged to go together the next morning in search of a French soldier.

To mark the day General de Gaulle, who had escaped from France only three weeks before, arranged a parade of his Free French Forces at the Cenotaph in Whitehall, and it was to this that Violette and Winnie went in the first instance. They saw representative detachments of many famous French regiments – sailors with red pompoms on their caps, young airmen in blue uniforms, soldiers carrying their rifles against their right shoulders, a corps of women in khaki tunics and smart forage caps, crews of French tanks in their distinctive padded helmets with a pistol in their belts, and smartest of all, they thought, the French Foreign Legion in steel helmets and white knitted scarves. In a motor-coach sat a group of wounded French soldiers in their hospital blue.

At ten o'clock precisely General de Gaulle arrived; tall, lean, impressive in his blue and gold kepi. He was received with round upon round of cheers from the troops, and the vast crowd of spectators joined in the ovation. Two steel-helmeted trumpeters then sounded a call and General de Gaulle laid a large laurel wreath at the foot of the Cenotaph. It was bound with the tricolor ribbon and bore the inscription *Les Français Libres.* Calling in a stentorian voice *"Salut aux Morts!"* the General came sharply to the salute. The French troops sprang to the salute too, and cried *"Vive la France … Vive Général de Gaulle."* They then marched to the statue of Marshal Foch in Grosvenor Gardens in Victoria where de Gaulle placed another wreath. So great was the excitement among the onlookers that France, as represented by these men and women, should still be in the fight with us, that they broke through the police cordons and mingled with the troops. Violette was too diffident to offer her invitation at such a moment, so she withdrew with Winnie for a snack at a nearby restaurant and then they went on to Hyde Park. There, seated on a bench at one of the intersecting paths, they glanced a little shyly at the passing soldiers and airmen, most of them British, a few Dutch, Polish or Norwegian. At last a French soldier came by. Neither girl was bold enough to take the lead in initiating a conversation. While they hesitated he was gone. But soon another came along, an officer of the French Foreign Legion. He glanced at them, particularly at Violette. Still neither girl spoke and he too was gone. But he did not go far. A few yards along he turned and came past them again. Then, taking the initiative himself, he addressed them. But he must have been a little shy too, for though he had been staring hard at Violette, it was to the other girl that he now spoke. What he said was in French, which Winnie did not understand at all. He said: "Pardon me, Mam'selle, but could you tell me what the time is?"

Violette, smiling as she drew his attention to the watch on his wrist, told him the time. He laughed, and with the ice thus broken, he asked if he might sit with them on the bench. The girls agreed. They talked together for a while, at least he talked to Violette, for he knew no English, and eventually it was he who issued an invitation. He asked the girls if they would care to have a cup of tea with him.

They accepted and over tea Violette, feeling she had by now got to know him, unfolded her mother's plan. The young French soldier was overjoyed, for it was becoming increasingly clear that he was deeply interested in Violette.

The girls took him back with them to Brixton. They entered the house in Burnley Road, but found it empty. Mr and Mrs Bushell were out. The three sat in the front lounge and talked till, hearing her parents return, Violette rushed to the front door and greeted her mother excitedly with the words: "Mummy, I have brought one home for you."

Her parents had no idea what she was talking about. "Come in and see," she urged them. As Mr and Mrs Bushell entered the lounge, the French soldier stood up, brought his heels together and bowed, announcing at the same time his name. It was Etienne Szabo.

He was of medium height, well-built and good-looking. His smile, they thought, was delightfully charming. One would have put his age at about thirty. He said he came from Marseilles, but Mrs Bushell was relieved to find that he did not have the Marseilles accent.

Mr and Mrs Bushell had been at a neighbour's where, remembering that Winston Churchill was broadcasting a Bastille Day message to France, they had tuned in to listen. They came home greatly impressed by what Churchill had said. He had raised their hopes and their spirits in what was a very dark hour.

"I proclaim my faith," he had said, "that some of us will live to see a Fourteenth of July when a liberated France will once again rejoice in her greatness and her glory, and once again stand forward as the champion of the freedom and the rights of man."

They talked of it all through dinner. They could talk of nothing else. Mrs Bushell tried to recall Churchill's words, and with Mr Bushell prompting, together they recaptured some of his phrases. "Britain," Churchill had said, "would so conduct itself in the war that every French heart would glow as every British victory brought them one step nearer to the liberation of the continent of Europe." With pride and with hope the small group round the Bushells' dining-table raised their glasses to the resurrection of France.

While they talked, both during dinner and after it, Mr and Mrs Bushell could not help noticing that Etienne Szabo kept glancing eagerly at Violette after every word, no matter who spoke it, in order to note her reaction. They noticed too, and this certainly surprised them, that Violette showed a responsive interest in him. It was as yet only an awakening of interest, but it was, for the first time to their knowledge, not the general lively interest which she normally showed, but a more concentrated interest, focused directly on one man.

Chapter 4

Etienne Szabo

Etienne Michel René Szabo was born on March 4th, 1910, at L'Estaque, which is practically a suburb of Marseilles. He was eleven years older than Violette, which made him thirty at their time of meeting. At five foot six he could not be considered tall, but he was more than three inches taller than her. His broad shoulders made him look a little stocky, but he had a fine oval face with well-chiselled features and could justly be considered good-looking. His smile was fascinating and the women thought him most attractive. Rather shy, yet lively and playful, he had a fund of anecdotes about his experiences and his travels.

His parents died when he was very young. His father had served in the gendarmerie in Marseilles and rose to the rank of captain. Etienne, seeking a career at the early age of sixteen, decided not to confine himself to wrestling with the vice and crime of his native city, but to venture further afield. He joined the French Foreign Legion and was sent out to North Africa. Dressed in the picturesque uniform of the Legionnaire, with leather straps crossed upon his chest, baggy trousers and a white kepi with its flowing linen *perruque,* he fought under the blistering sun of the desert shoulder to shoulder with men from a dozen countries – Norway, Sweden, Belgium and even Germany, some of them fugitives from justice, others soured by life or jilted by a girl, a few merely adventurous in spirit. They were drilled and disciplined and welded into an astonishingly fine fighting force.

Etienne Szabo already had behind him a dozen years of

fighting. He had been in action in Algiers, Tunis and Morocco against wild and merciless tribesmen and had even fought as far afield as Syria and Indo-China. He had been wounded and his breast was abundantly decorated. To Violette, as the exploits were unfolded with a pleasing diffidence, he must have seemed a sort of P.C. Wren hero such as she had seen in *Beau Geste* on the screen. He had endured hardships and faced perils that roused her own stout spirit. These were the things she would have liked to have done too. With him in the Foreign Legion as his captain was that great French soldier General Koenig, who, when France fell, rowed across the Channel in a fishing boat, was raised to the rank of General by de Gaulle and was in command, as it happened, of the section of the Free French forces with which Etienne was now serving in England.

The outbreak of war in 1939 did not immediately involve the French Foreign Legion. They waited through the tedious months of the phoney war, wondering where and when they might be used. It was not till November that they left Africa for France. Arriving at Marseilles they had a night or two in Etienne's old familiar haunts in that city, then they were moved to a camp at Larzac and trained on the slopes to fight surprisingly on skis, for they were to be sent to Finland to assist that little country in its grim struggle for survival against the armed hordes of Russia. But before they were ready, Finland capitulated. Early in April 1940, when Germany surged northwards through Denmark and Quisling's Fifth Column brought Norway under German domination, the Legionnaires got ready once more to fight amid the snows of the Arctic.

Etienne sailed from Brest for England on April 22nd and joined the Allied expedition about to cross the North Sea. The plan was to stop the advancing Germans at Trondheim, about halfway up the Norwegian coast. But, finding the Germans too strongly entrenched there, the expedition went on to Narvik, in the extreme north, where the position looked more hopeful. Here, together with a strong British contingent which included the Scots Guards, the Irish Guards and the Welsh Borderers, the French Foreign Legion, numbering close on a thousand officers and men, were landed and were joined by the Chasseurs Alpins. To these two famous French regiments a young Scots Greys Captain was attached as British liaison officer. His name was Geoffrey Keyes and he was to win undying fame the following year by his daring raid on Rommel's headquarters two hundred miles behind the enemy lines in North Africa. There incidentally Etienne Szabo was also to go fairly soon. Geoffrey Keyes was awarded the Victoria Cross posthumously. At Narvik, with Etienne, he shared the fortunes and perils of the French Foreign Legion.

The country was wild and mountainous. A fierce wind whipped the snow into their faces and howled hideously in their ears as the Allied troops and what remained of the Norwegian Army launched attack after attack on skis. They fought against overwhelming odds. They were short of ammunition and equipment. German planes bombed them by night and by day with hardly any aircraft of our own to prevent them. Rations were often inadequate and, through a lack of billets, many slept in the open and suffered severely from exposure. The Foreign Legion in particular sustained very heavy casualties. There were incredible escapes. But they acquitted themselves well, for French morale, here at any rate, was high.

While the fight for Narvik was still in progress, the Germans at dawn on May 10th launched their attack on Western Europe. Swarms of troops rained down by parachute on Holland, Belgium and on France, ahead of the advancing panzer divisions which were supported by tanks and by planes. Soon all was confusion. By a circling move to the coast the Germans trapped the bulk of the British Army. The evacuation from Dunkirk followed. The attempt to capture Narvik was thereupon abandoned and a similar and almost simultaneous evacuation was begun there. In destroyers and transports the various regiments were brought back from Norway to the Clyde. Here on June 13th Etienne and the remnants of the Foreign Legion were landed, suffering from frostbite and fatigue. The Germans entered Paris the next day

31

and France fell little more than a week later. De Gaulle, however, refused to accept defeat. Defying the policy of Marechal Pétain, who was shortly to establish his Government at Vichy, he jumped into a plane and came to England to carry on the fight.

Some of the French troops brought back from Narvik to England insisted on repatriation, but Etienne preferred to stay on and volunteered for service with the Free French Forces of de Gaulle. He was sent to Liverpool for his training, was given a new uniform, British made, with the proud Cross of Lorraine, the emblem of the Free French, on the lapel. With thousands more of his countrymen he marched and drilled under the changed mechanised requirements of modern warfare. On the eve of Bastille Day he was sent up to London for the parade with a small group of Legionnaires. They were housed in the vast Exhibition Hall at Olympia and granted a few days' leave before joining their new regiment at Aldershot. It was his good fortune, he considered, that on his very first day off he should have met Violette and, seated around the table with her family, was able to converse so freely in his native tongue. Orphaned in childhood and detached for many years from any such setting, it gave him a pleasant sense of belonging. From the start he seemed to merge into the warmth of their friendliness.

They talked for hours after dinner and it became increasingly clear that it was his intention to see Violette again both on the next day and on the day after that – until in fact the time came for him to go to Aldershot.

It was very late when he left that night. The Bushells were not at all sure that he hadn't missed his last bus back. But he regarded that as immaterial. Saying good night at the door he kissed Violette's hand a little too fervently perhaps, and asked, shyly, half apologetically, if she would show him something of London.

She smiled, flushed a little and agreed at once. Her parents exchanged understanding glances and the young pair were thus launched within a few hours of their meeting upon a whirlwind courtship.

To the Bushells, as they talked about him later in their back bedroom, he seemed quite a desirable young man. He had a pleasing personality, a gay manner, and was keenly intelligent. True, he had made the army his career, but so for that matter had Mr Bushell, and they did not see anything wrong in that. He was an officer with a blaze of ribbons on his breast and a fine fighting record. He would, they felt, undoubtedly go far: one never knew but he might even by the end of the war attain the exalted rank of colonel. Violette, they knew, was not disposed to marry yet: indeed she had said on her return from Fareham, only a day or two before, that she had no intention of marrying until she was twenty-five, and that was six years away. None the less they speculated on the possible developments and indulged in the luxury of visualising their daughter living in Algiers or Tunis, visiting Casablanca, Rabat and Marrakesh, and retiring with her colonel to a small villa either in Paris or just outside it, honoured, respected by her neighbours, and with a young family around her.

Etienne met her in town the following afternoon. They went for a bus ride to Richmond, had tea there and spent the evening at the Academy Cinema, seeing a French film – just opposite the branch of Woolworth's where she used to work before the war. The next night he came to Brixton for dinner. Not many of the family were at home now. Roy had joined the army and was at Aldershot where Etienne had every intention of seeing him. John, now in his sixteenth year, had recently joined the Engineers. The two younger boys had been evacuated to the country. Grandma Bushell went up early to bed. So when the parents tactfully left the front lounge, Violette and Etienne had it to themselves.

For the end of the week Violette arranged a little outing. Into it she drew her friend Winnie Wilson and asked Etienne if he could bring someone to form a foursome. He arrived at Brixton for lunch, with a young French soldier named Marcel, who also, alas, could speak no English. So on Violette all three had to rely for inter-communication.

After the meal they left for Hyde Park by bus. It was a beautiful July day, warm and sunny. They reclined in deck-

33

chairs and talked for a while. Poor Winnie could see the others laughing and jesting without being able to participate in it. At intervals Violette supplied a synopsised translation, but in this form, unshared, it did not appear to be funny. So they abandoned their chatter, hired a boat and went rowing on the Serpentine. Violette was good at it and won approving glances from Etienne, and Marcel too was ungrudging in his commendation. They had tea afterwards at Lyons' Corner House at Marble Arch and, walking to the bus stop, Etienne bought her an enormous bunch of roses from a barrow. Marcel followed his example and Winnie accepted his offering entirely in dumb show. Through consideration for her, they went to see an English film at the New Victoria, and Violette now had to do the interpreting for the men. This was actually Etienne's last day in town. His leave had come to an end and the following morning he left for Aldershot. He had promised, however, to write, and within twenty-four hours his first letter arrived at Brixton. He also saw to it that the link was maintained by more than the exchange of letters, for one of the first things he did on arriving at Aldershot was to call and make himself known to Violette's brother Roy.

Violette wrote to Roy. Roy wrote to Violette. Every day Etienne and Violette wrote long letters to each other. She stayed in now in the evenings to write to him and to read his letters through again and again. After a few days, since Aldershot was only thirty-five miles away, quite suddenly Etienne came up to spend an hour or so with her. Then Violette declared a day or two later that it was high time the family went down to see Roy. But before she could arrange it, Etienne came up again with twenty-four hours' leave and Mrs Bushell gave him a shake-down for the night on the settee in the sitting-room. Breathlessly the young pair told each other again the many things they had said already in their letters.

Soon things began to move swiftly. His regiment was under orders to go abroad. Pressure was at once applied by Violette on the family, who realised suddenly that it was now most urgent for them to go down and see Roy. At the last minute Mrs Bushell was unable to come, but Violette insisted that her father should accompany her. They were met at the station by both Etienne and Roy. What puzzled Mr Bushell was Etienne's strange behaviour. Etienne had apparently learned a word or two of English and was intent on trying them out on him, since no conversation in French was possible with Mr Bushell. But words like 'very good' and 'yes' cannot get one very far and, having said them, Etienne, aware of Violette's watchful eye on him, took refuge in a sort of shy laughter. He remained, however, by Mr Bushell's side and on a sudden inspiration walked him on briskly ahead of the others. This was neither to Mr Bushell's taste nor understanding. He kept turning round to inquire in an ever louder voice, as Violette and Roy lagged further and further behind, what on earth Etienne was trying to say in a very carefully mouthed and precise French, interspersed with the few irrelevant and entirely out-of-place words of English he had acquired.

But Violette was not very helpful. She seemed suddenly unable to translate. One might have surmised from this what was in Etienne's mind, but Mr Bushell remained bewildered and was quite astonished when he was taken to a remote bench and asked if he would mind sitting down for a little talk. Mysteriously at that precise moment Violette and Roy disappeared from sight.

Mr Bushell sat down and gazed about him in wonder. Etienne remained standing. He cleared his throat, straightened his tie, and poured out a volley in fast French, which was of course completely beyond Mr Bushell's comprehension. Papa looked round again for Violette, and even called to her, but she seemed to be nowhere. About to rise, he was thrust back into his seat. Etienne, straightening his tie again, began again. This time he decided to rely almost entirely on gestures. He pointed to where Violette had last been seen, placed his hand on his heart, and rolled his eyes, from all of which Mr Bushell gathered that it must be a declaration of love and that Etienne was asking for Papa's consent to their marriage.

It took Mr Bushell completely by surprise. He had been aware that a romance was developing, but he did not expect a proposal quite so soon. They had only known each other for two weeks. Less than a month ago Violette was saying that she had no intention of getting married until she was twenty-five – then along comes this fellow and bowls her completely over. Come to think of it, they didn't really know very much about him. Mr Bushell frowned as he reflected on all this, then, his mind made up, he said, speaking of course in English: "I think she is far too young. She's only nineteen, you know."

It was Etienne's turn now to look for a translator. Surprisingly Violette was near enough to have heard, for at that moment she emerged from behind some trees barely a yard or two away.

Turning to her father she fixed him with a determined eye. "Daddy," she said, "you either give your consent or I shall marry Etienne without it."

It was clear that his consent was no more than a formality with which, as a Frenchman, Etienne felt it was important to conform. Papa shrugged his shoulders. Before he could say anything the young couple were clasped in each other's arms.

Etienne insisted on going there and then to buy a large bunch of roses for her. The ring he already had in his pocket – it had a square emerald surrounded by diamonds. With a smile he slipped it on to the appropriate finger. Over lunch the talk was largely concerned with plans for the wedding. Etienne's regiment was to sail within three weeks and the wedding would obviously have to be within the next week or so.

The date selected was Wednesday, August 21st, and Aldershot was the obvious place for it. But before then Etienne came up to town for a day and was shown off to the Buckinghams and the girls at the Bon Marché. "She was so proud of him," says Miss Bird, manageress of the department Violette had been working in not many weeks before. "She hung on to his arm all the time she was in the shop."

Only Mr and Mrs Bushell were able to go down for the wedding and Roy was there too, of course. Violette looked extremely pretty in a dark high-necked dress, a pull-on trilby-style hat and a belted camel coat. Etienne, wearing a khaki béret slightly tipped over his right ear, looked handsome and debonair. They were honoured by the presence of General Koenig himself, who had known Etienne since his earliest years in the Foreign Legion. Tall, lean, with a high-bridged nose and a small moustache, he was magnificently impressive and played the role not only of commanding officer, but almost of a father. About twenty men from the regiment came to the ceremony. Lieutenant Etienne Kiss was best man.

But they had no sooner assembled at the registrar's than the air-raid sirens went and they all had to troop out again, as the regulations required, and take refuge in the nearest shelter. There the bridal party sat uncomfortably on long hard benches facing each other. Violette held Etienne's hand and wrinkled her nose as she smiled up at him. Roy made facetious jests and each of the French soldiers in turn had a jibe of some sort at the expense of bride and bridegroom. They sat there for nearly two hours. It was for the young couple an agonising wait. They could hear the guns.

Quite a heavy fire was being directed at enemy planes. But no bombs were dropped and no planes were brought down.

At last with a sigh of relief they heard the All Clear and returned to the registrar's. It was a war-time austerity wedding and, not being in France, there were no accordions and no singing and dancing. But there was champagne and a large meal to tuck into. General Koenig kissed the bride, then honoured the bridegroom by kissing him on both cheeks. He next approached Mr Bushell, who nervously expected to be kissed too, but got only a handshake. Mrs Bushell's fingers were raised to the General's lips. Toasts were drunk and amid a great deal of hilarity and laughter photographs were taken. When the bride is beautiful, cameramen never fail to appear, but this was also an international occasion. A Free French soldier had married an English girl after a very brief courtship. Since Etienne could not speak to the reporters except in French, Violette told them proudly of his heroism in many battles in Morocco, Syria and Indo-China, of his wounds, of his decorations. Etienne's wedding gift to her was a very beautiful gold bracelet.

The honeymoon had necessarily to be brief. It was spent at a small hotel just outside Aldershot. A few days later Etienne sailed with his regiment and Violette returned to the home of her parents in Brixton.

Chapter 5

Brief Homecoming

For Violette, after the lively developments of the past five weeks, everything – her thoughts, her outlook, life itself – had changed. But the cause of the change was no longer with her and there was an emptiness all around. No more the quick exchange of letters, of hearing the bell and finding him at the front door with an armful of roses; no hurrying to catch a train to join him. Every day in fact bore him further and further away to some vague and Heaven knew what destiny.

Etienne was travelling many thousands of miles round the Cape and up the east coast of Africa. No direct passage through the Mediterranean was any longer possible. Mussolini, having come into the war on June 10th, when the fate of France was clearly sealed, had embarked on his cherished dream of establishing a new Roman Empire around the Mediterranean. He had large armies already in position for the fulfilment of this purpose – in Abyssinia, in Eritrea, in Somaliland and on the frontier of Egypt, and had the satisfaction of knowing that no French army from Tunis could any longer attack him from the rear. His aircraft, and Nazi aircraft too, had for the time being almost the whole of the Mediterranean at their mercy.

Even before Etienne and the French contingent sailed Mussolini's forces had begun to move in each of these scattered fields of operation. To which of them Etienne was being sent even he did not know. He wrote long letters home to his wife and sent numerous postcards to Mr and Mrs Bushell, to Roy and even to aunts and cousins such as the Buckinghams at Harmondsworth and the Lucases at Hereford. The cards came from Durban and from Eritrea – a simple sepia landscape for Mama, a half-nude native girl reading a book for young John Buckingham with *'Mes meilleurs souvenirs et une bonne poignée de main. A bientôt.'* To them, because of the difficulty over his Christian name, he was known as Stephen. All the place-names were struck out, and the scenes remained unidentified, but a hint of the setting was conveyed in his references to *'ce pays très chaud'* and his longings – *'Je rêve d'un demi de bière bien glacé'.* It was at Asmara that his regiment was ultimately landed and they made their way southwards to deal with the Italians in Abyssinia.

For Violette the solace of occasional, overdue cards and letters that arrived in batches was scarcely enough. She had to fill the emptiness with work – and yet Etienne had specifically stated that he did not want her to do any work at all. He was doing the fighting. He wanted her to live quietly at home as befitted the wife of a French officer. The allowance the Free French Army made her of five pounds a week should be sufficient for this purpose, he felt. She tried to adhere to his wishes – indeed it was her intention when he left to observe them to the letter – but she found it impossible to sit idly at home fretting, brooding. So after some weeks she took a job as a telephonist at a new automatic exchange in the City located in one of the numerous alleyways that existed then around St Paul's Cathedral. The air assault on London opened at about the same time. The Battle of Britain, begun early in July and fought chiefly above the countryside around London, leaving white streaks across the sky like ski trails, had by now been lost by the Germans, and they sent their planes to vent their wrath upon London, which it was their resolve to paralyse and if possible destroy. Indiscriminate bombing of the metropolis began early in September. Punctually as darkness fell each night the bombers came, at times they came also by day. Through it all, like millions more, Violette carried on with her work. A shelter to her was anathema, nothing would induce her to use it. She went out quite unconcernedly at night through the heaviest raids, usually to the cinema, occasionally with Winnie to the Locarno at Streatham. In this richly decorated dance hall, with its soft lights and encircling balcony, they would sit over a drink or a coffee and listen to famous entertainers like Adelaide Hall and Jessie Matthews singing to the troops, and they would dance to such tunes as *So Deep is the Night*, *Begin the Beguine*, *The White Cliffs of Dover*, and inevitably at the time *Run, Rabbit, Run*. The place had a lively, cheerful atmosphere which helped one to forget the grim times through which one was living. Winnie recalls occasions when they had to stay at the Locarno all night because no transport could be found while the raid was on. To the clatter of shrapnel falling on the Locarno roof Violette remained of course indifferent, smoking, chatting, having more coffee and, when the dawn came, going back with Winnie to have tea in her sitting-room in front of a roaring fire.

Almost every morning fresh bomb damage was revealed all round them: windows had been blown out, houses lay in heaps of rubble, ambulances waited and search-parties dug in the debris for people buried beneath it. One morning in December, walking along Stockwell Road, Violette saw a scene of great disorder round her old school. The road was cordoned off in front. A part of the old drab building had been burnt out, leaving charred ruins against the grey sky. Where her old classroom had been there was now a gaping void. A single oil incendiary bomb had done all this damage. Three weeks later it was the place where she worked that lay in ruins, for on the night of Sunday, December 29th, 1940, the German air force made a concentrated attack upon the City. Most of the water mains were burst open by the initial assault. There then followed a downpour of land mines which left a vast wreckage, destroying entire streets, skeletonising many lovely Wren churches and damaging even the Guildhall. By a miracle St Paul's Cathedral escaped, though all around it there was the greatest devastation.

Violette and the other girls working at the telephone exchange were given a few weeks off until new premises could be found. The exchange was eventually housed in such accommodation as was available – a cold, damp cellar in which the girls had often to sit on the floor. But they carried on.

Violette was more than ever resolved now to join one of the Services. The one she had in mind was the ATS, but her mother insisted that Etienne should first be consulted. He had apparently accepted her being at the telephone exchange, though one could not say that he approved of it. But there was no doubt in either of their minds that he would be livid when he learned of her being exposed for many hours of the day, and often also the night, to the damp and the cold of this cellar. As for her going into one of the Services, well – Mama just shrugged and reminded her that in every letter of late he spoke of coming home in the summer and it was obvious that he would not want, while here on very short leave, to find her posted at the other end of Scotland. None the less Violette wrote as her mother had suggested. She wanted, she said, to take a much more active part in the war. There was, she felt, something worthwhile she could do. She hoped he would feel the same way about it.

While awaiting his reply, she took a hacking cough she had developed in the cellar on a brief spell of convalescence at her Aunt Florence's place in Hereford. She had a lively time there. Her cousin Norman was home on leave and they went careering together all over the countryside on his motor-bike, with her clinging on behind. She had barely got back from this brief respite when a telegram from Liverpool informed her that Etienne was home. She packed hurriedly and caught: the first train out, impatient to be with him again.

It was a great thrill to be reunited. His sudden homecoming, without weeks of anticipatory waiting, made it all the pleasanter. After a year under the tropical sun, Etienne looked bronzed and exceedingly fit. He had, he revealed, been fighting in Abyssinia. It had been a long and victorious campaign and he had emerged from it unscathed. The Emperor had been restored to this throne in May, and the Allied units there had been moved to the north to partake in the Western Desert battles. Auchinleck had by now taken over from Wavell, who became Viceroy of India. On the other side stood Rommel, who had won his reputation by his swift sweep across the Somme and in the fighting all round Abbeville and Pont Rémy where

Violette had played as a child. Most of the desert wrested from the Italians by Wavell had been recovered recently by Rommel. A great battle was obviously in the offing and in this Etienne was to be engaged when he returned from his leave of only seven days.

But neither of them wanted to think of the war now. Etienne knew Liverpool well, for he had been training there for some weeks on his return from Narvik. He engaged a luxurious room in one of the best hotels and they embarked on a second honeymoon. They dined in restaurants, went to the theatre and went dancing. It was an ecstatic week, but, dread it though they both did, inevitably the morning came for their goodbye. He returned by plane to Cairo and she had to try and settle down again to the humdrum round of life without him.

But she had extracted his consent to join the ATS and, on arriving in London, went straight on to the recruiting office in Victoria to join up.

The war had now become for her much more fierce and personal. A vital part of her was closely involved in it – had been returned for a moment and was then snatched away again. They had talked a great deal of what their life would be after it was all over. He had said: "I want to take you to Paris, which you can't remember really, as you were only a child. And we will go together to the Madeleine to give thanks for our survival – that is, if I survive." He had added this with a smile, and she had kissed him fervently to reassure herself and him: of course he would survive, she could not bear to contemplate the alternative. They had talked also of having a family and had argued playfully over the number of girls and boys there should be. And now he was gone, many thousands and thousands of miles away, to fight with who knew what outcome.

Chapter 6

With the Ack-Ack Battery

Violette joined the ATS on September 11th, 1941. She got her first uniform and, though only a private, was proud of the opportunity it gave her to serve. After being put through all the processes that recruits have to endure, but without a rifle, for girls were not allowed them, she was sent on to Leicester, where she had lived as a child of eight, not quite a dozen years before. Parts of the town were consequently familiar to her. She had been to a local council school, one of her very first in England, and she had been in and out of the shops with her mother. Now, with the other girls in the ATS, she enjoyed a number of evening diversions and dances, especially arranged for men and women in the forces.

The work she was called upon to do did not particularly appeal to her. It consisted of the usual chores that are assigned to women, such as cooking, waiting at table and attending to the laundry. She had heard, however, of a plan for using women in anti-aircraft batteries, not on the guns, but to aid and direct the guns by operating predictors, height-finders, and other instruments. An experiment along these lines had in fact been started not many weeks before in view of the increasing shortage of men. It was regarded as successful and women were accordingly invited to volunteer for such work. Violette was among the first to join. She felt in a way that she was following in the footsteps of her father, who had begun his military career as a gunner in the Royal Horse Artillery.

The battery to which Violette was posted was Battery No. 481 (M). It was under the command of Major J.W. Naylor, who had himself served, like Mr Bushell, in the RHA. He went to France on the outbreak of the Second World War, returned shortly before Dunkirk and was given command of an anti-aircraft battery in western Scotland, where enemy attacks were constant and lively. His appointment now to take charge of a mixed battery was not at all to his taste. He did not welcome having under his control 'a bunch of giggling females', as he phrased it, and regarded it as hardly the way an old soldier could be expected to serve his King and country. To us now this attitude may seem old-fashioned and stuffy, but it should be remembered that girls had not, save in this recent experiment, been used yet in active warfare with artillery. Those who then knew Jim Naylor would stoutly deny that he had in him even a hint of the blimp mentality: for one thing he was only in his early forties, and they knew that behind his keen efficiency lay a light-hearted and jovial personality; and to them at any rate it was not surprising that, after he had worked with the girls and had begun to know them, he should develop a regard and even an admiration for their enthusiasm and skill. "There was no hardship the men faced that the girls weren't prepared to endure," he says. "Their devotion to duty was really remarkable and I found that, though slow starters at everything that was technical, they became in time just as efficient as the men."

The battery, composed entirely of recruits, was assembled at Oswestry in Shropshire, in the third week of October 1941. The girls outnumbered the men. Some, like Violette, were shop girls, others were secretaries or had worked in factories; there were also children's nurses and school teachers with university degrees. Others had come straight from their homes. A few were married – one was the mother of four children. Such was the raw material Naylor had to train and shape into an efficient fighting unit. He was aware that critical eyes were upon them, watchful for such embarrassments as might arise from the close association of large numbers of men and women, who, besides working together, were to share their hours of relaxation and diversion. The position was undoubtedly delicate. Wisely he laid down no stern and rigid restrictions, but decided to deal with eventualities as they arose. He was greatly assisted in this by Junior Commander Vida Torry and her two ATS subalterns Blanche Johnson and Diana Hewitt, who always ignored irregularities that seemed to be merely departures from normal army standards and accepted the laughter, the gaiety and the good humour as part of the more varied life of a mixed unit.

Adjustments also had to be made in the attitude of the men. The battery sergeant-major, for example, on being told that the ATS officers ought to be addressed as 'ma'am', decided to ignore the direction. He felt outraged at the very presence of women in the camp and declined to admit even to himself that they were there. So whenever one of the ATS officers addressed him, he sprang to attention, saluted and said: "Yes, sir." Naylor had a long talk with him about this, but it made no difference. Every woman officer remained 'sir' to him until the end of the war.

Violette attracted unwittingly a great deal of attention from the outset. The impression seemed to have got around that she was really a member of the Free French Forces, to which her slight French accent lent some colour. There were whispers that she had contrived to come out of enemy occupied France, had undergone many adventures and had some very narrow escapes. In their eyes she became in consequence something of a heroine, but she soon dispelled this by informing them that it was her husband who was serving with the Free French and that she herself was only half French and had been free anyway. She sought neither the glamour nor the glory of the heroine. They were drawn to her by her frankness and modesty and liked her because, as one of them says, she was gay, vivacious, intelligent and very pretty. She had a great sense of fun. Her eyes used to dance with mischief when the thought of playing a prank came into her head. They were innocent pranks, schoolgirlish in fact, as, for instance, when she put her foot on the fire hose and, just as the sergeant-major peered into the nozzle, threatened to lift her foot and let the water spurt right into his face.

They had Nissen huts to live in, the girls segregated in one group, the men in another. But in the general canteen there was no such separation. The good-natured chipping between the sexes soon developed into a warmth and friendliness, and after supper, if a mobile film unit or ENSA entertainers were not visiting them, they danced or put on an improvised show.

The exaggerated hip movements of the girls on parade, which made them rather like a musical comedy chorus, were corrected and they were sent out on long route marches. All wore trousers, always scrupulously well creased; lipstick was only allowed off duty; and the canteen now carried an extra line of hair nets, vanishing cream and other feminine requirements.

A series of early tests revealed what each girl was best fitted for. Some were made cooks, others were put on to clerical and administrative work. Violette was not only relieved but highly excited when she was selected to work a Vickers predictor. It would give her a chance to make a direct contribution. The bombing she had experienced in London she would now be able to answer. Working in a team of six girls, of whom she was quite the smallest, she could barely reach the telescope and appeared always to be standing on tiptoe while operating her predictor. None the less she proved to be extremely good at following the target and always got the men right on the mark. This and other indications of her efficiency finally dispelled the doubts at first entertained by Naylor as to whether a girl so small and light-hearted would make a good soldier. At his weekly inspections he always found her smart in appearance, her bed and her kit were well looked after and beautifully laid out. "She was more pains-taking, more eager to please, than the rest," he says, "and my pats on the back made her flush with gratification. She was unselfish in the extreme. The team spirit was strong in her. Girls in her unit who were in need of her guidance were shown by her just how their own things should be attended to, with the result that her hut was the best kept of all the huts in the battery – and I include in that all the men's huts as well.

"She was a gay little thing and her gaiety was most infectious. In whatever we were doing, in every new phase of the battery's life and its varied activities, Violette was always the leading light. Yet she never pushed herself forward or tried in any way to be regarded as better than the rest. Whatever had to be done she was eager that they should all do it together and that it should really be done well.

"She had, it will be seen from this, despite her gaiety, both an earnestness and a sense of purpose. She was aware that the times were grim, that tragedy had touched many millions of lives in Britain, in France and elsewhere on the continent of Europe. That same menace hung over her husband and so far over two of her brothers.

"She was particularly proud of her husband. She asked me whether, in view of the fact that he was fighting with the Free French Forces, she might be allowed to wear the Free French flash on the shoulders of her battle-dress blouse. Permission to do this was obtained and when the flashes were sewn on, one detected a sort of swagger as she swung her shoulders while moving about the camp.

"She made friends easily. Her comrades in the battery had come from all sorts of homes, many of them extremely humble, like her own. Violette was friendly with all of them, not only the other girls on operational jobs, but even with those who were cooks, drivers, telephonists and clerks."

She wrote and told Etienne of all this, her letters not quite so long now, but still full of amusing details. He was back in the Western Desert, getting ready to take part in the long-awaited offensive against Rommel. Inexplicably the attack kept on being deferred, although, with the Germans so heavily engaged on their Eastern front ever since they plunged into war with Russia, it seemed undoubtedly a good time to strike. But not until the middle of November was the attack at last launched. Our blow had immense weight and we made some headway. But within three days Rommel counter-attacked and drove us all the way back. Our tanks seemed to be no match for the Germans. We suffered a series of reverses and for a time even the safety of Egypt was at stake. Rommel was, however, halted eventually and the tide was turned suddenly in our favour. Tobruk, still held by us in the heart of enemy-occupied territory, was relieved. Rommel stopped to lick his wounds and there followed a gratifying pause. But one realised that soon, inevitably, it would all flare up again.

Early in December, by the Japanese attack on Pearl Harbour, the war was extended to many new fronts and a powerful ally, America, was brought in on our side.

All through the autumn the weather at Oswestry had steadily worsened. It became bitterly cold. Snow lay thick on the ground. Often it rained heavily and the girls marched with their hair hanging in rats' tails.

After some weeks of this the battery was sent to a practice camp at Anglesey where their operational skill was put to the test. Using their predictors and radar location, the girls assisted the gunners to aim at aerial targets towed by planes. The weather there too was appalling, but nothing damped their ardour, least of all Violette's. The camp commandant, greatly pleased with their progress, granted them extended home leave before putting them on operations. Violette returned to the parental home in Brixton and had a month to go about and see her friends. She saw Winnie of course and went to the Bon Marché to show off her uniform to the girls. Eager questions were asked about Etienne and promises were extracted that he would be brought there again on his next home-coming.

The battery reassembled at Crewe station a week before Christmas and moved on to join the Mersey anti-aircraft defences in one of the most active bombing areas in the country. One half of the battery was stationed at Alvanley, the rest, Violette among them, at Sutton Weaver, seven miles away. They had an air raid to deal with on their very first night.

Coming for the first time into a fully operational area a new unit is apt, possibly through a nervous over-eagerness, to run into certain unforeseen difficulties, such as giving a false alarm of enemy raiders overhead. It brought most of the Mersey defences into action with nothing to hit at. There followed inevitably a good deal of bitter sarcasm, but Violette took it all with her customary cheerfulness. Her jesting at moments of stress, without a sign of fluster or concern, happily proved infectious and helped to allay the misgivings of the battery commander as to the girls' ability to face up to real danger. Violette's behaviour, he states, had an admirable effect. The exclamatory gasps and shrieks, the loud-voiced *ooh*-ing and

49

aah-ing to which girls are so often addicted, slowly gave place to a more orderly, one might almost say a disciplined, good humour.

As an example of her comradeship and influence on the others, he cites the occasion when one of the girls, an ATS spotter, seeing an unfamiliar type of plane overhead, sounded the alarm. Both Britain and the Germans, he states, had new types of aircraft which closely resembled each other. The alarm brought them all to action stations and just as they were about to fire, the error was detected. An inquiry was ordered and the distress of the ATS spotter was great. But Violette allayed her fears. "You cannot be blamed for doing what you considered was right," she reassured her. "It might easily have been an enemy plane, and it was your duty to report it."

The brigade commander, Brigadier V.R. Krohn, came down to the gun site. Violette, standing with the others, watched the frightened little spotter as, trembling a little, she came before him. She glanced quickly towards Violette. The other girls stole a glance at her too, as though half expecting her to intervene. But the brigade commander was understanding and just. After listening to the girl's halting explanation, he congratulated her on acting so promptly on her suspicions. Her face flushed in relief; once again she turned to Violette as though to say, "You were right! I need not have worried after all." Incidents of this kind reveal the tremendous popularity Violette enjoyed and the confidence she radiated.

The alarm went almost every night. They rushed from their beds, their eyes heavy with sleep. Often, struggling into their coats as they ran, they stumbled and fell into a cabbage patch in the darkness. Once, arriving during a raid, the battery commander, Major Naylor, saw Violette busy at her predictor, dressed in pale blue pyjamas and a pair of red slippers; from her shoulders hung her greatcoat; on the back of her head was perched her tin hat. At times the action lasted for three hours or more. The girls at the instruments had no cover at all and were liable to be hit by a falling bomb and by shell splinters – indeed one girl working a predictor in another battery was killed shortly afterwards in this manner.

Their time off was admirably divided between sport and other diversions. At first the girls kept to basketball and netball, but later they joined the men in their games of soccer. The evening dances were lively, but quite the gayest and most hilarious of their diversions were the concerts they put on themselves. Violette took part in almost all of them, singing at times (she had a pleasant little voice), or acting in some of the sketches, but often it was a solo dance of her own evolution, with exotic and acrobatic touches that were excruciatingly funny.

Not only on the stage was she diverting. Elsie Bean says: "Violette was always in the lead when it came to fun. She worked hard and she played hard. She was full of vitality. She always had to be doing something. I remember she started a class to teach us all French." She had to get the battery commander's permission to do that. It proved a most successful venture – men as well as girls went to it. They got both instruction and diversion.

The battery came to be regarded as a model one and there was a constant flow of visitors. The GOC-in-C, General Pile, came down to inspect them. Shortly afterwards Miss Rosita Forbes, well known for her travels in the Near East, in Afghanistan and in India, spent a few days with them so that she might refer to their work in the course of the lecture tour she was about to undertake in America. There followed a host of journalists and press photographers from London. The BBC sent a recording van and arranged a broadcast which showed the girls at work and at play, with a singsong in the canteen as the finale.

Early the following April Junior Commander Vida Torry, the battery's senior ATS officer, reported to Major Naylor that Violette had asked for her discharge as she was expecting a baby. Naylor says: "I had a chat with her before she left. She was of course very excited about having a baby. She had heard that her husband would be getting leave soon and returning from Libya to be with her. She hated leaving the battery – that was obvious – but she had no choice. She promised to keep in touch with us and to return as soon as her baby was old enough

51

to be left. But long before that Violette volunteered for far more perilous duties.

"The battery was most distressed at the prospect of losing her, for she had become quite a personality in our small circle. But that she would come back none of us believed. A few, surprisingly enough, seemed to feel that she would be going on to do bigger and even heroic things. But of this, I am quite sure, she herself was completely unaware at the time."

Shortly after she left, the battery was moved to the gun site in Hyde Park in London and was visited there by the King and Queen, by Field-Marshal Smuts, and many times by Winston Churchill, the Prime Minister, whose daughter Mary had joined it by now as a subaltern.

Chapter 7

Tania

Her mother and father were, of course, greatly excited at her news and looked forward with an ecstatic eagerness to the arrival of their first grandchild. They had filled Violette's room with flowers for her home-coming and insisted on her having breakfast in bed for the first few days at any rate, since she was not prepared to let her mother wait on her. Noel, the third of her brothers, had gone into the Navy a few months before on reaching the age of fifteen. Dickie, seven now, was still in Hereford with Aunt Florence, away from the bombing, and Grandma Bushell had gone to live there too. So, with the two elder boys already in the services, there were only her parents at home now.

She had written to tell Etienne the joyous news as soon as she was sure, but with the delays to which their letters were subjected, it was only now that his reply reached her. He was overjoyed. He intended, he said, to do his damnedest to be with her when the time came. 'Don't be surprised,' he wrote, 'if you find me standing at the door one afternoon when you answer the bell.' He told her to find a place that could be a home for the three of them. A flat, he felt, would not be difficult to get, with London so empty. She had herself felt this would be the best course. Despite all the kindness her mother would shower on them and the discomforts her parents would gladly put themselves to, there was really not very much room in the Brixton house even with the boys away. She did not want her child to have the narrow, confined setting that she had herself known in her childhood. Things were easier now. There was the money from Etienne which the Free French paid her regularly. She talked it over with Mama, who agreed that it would be best from every point of view if she got a flat of her own.

Violette set out eagerly on the quest. She wanted it to be in town, for, although the child could not be kept there, or in Brixton for that matter, while the bombing continued, it would be better for her and for Etienne while he was on what would inevitably be a very brief spell of leave, to have it near the West End. She went first to Bayswater, which she knew well during the months she had lived there as a child. Not far from their old home, in a wide street known as Pembridge Villas, which sweeps towards Notting Hill Gate, she found a small and attractive flat and for some weeks she was pleasantly employed in furnishing it. Going from store to store, though furniture was not too plentiful, she got, mostly on hire purchase, beds and tables, settees, carpets and china.

The time of her confinement drew near. The child was expected very early in June. But there was no news of Etienne's home-coming. She knew from the newspapers something of what was going on in the desert, though not of course in how much of it Etienne was involved. The glorious successes achieved by Auchinleck in November had forced the enemy back to Gazala and eventually to El Agheila. But towards the end of January 1942 Rommel had managed again to win back most of the ground. There followed a pause. But, at the end of May, Rommel struck again.

During the first week of June she went into St Mary's Hospital in Paddington, and there on the 8th her child was born – a girl, small and dark as she herself was, and very like her, everyone said, but with just a look of Etienne. She named the child Tania.

Soon after leaving the hospital, urged not to keep the child too long in a bombing area, Violette took Tania down to Havant, not far from Fareham, where she had been working on the land during the first summer of the war. She had heard that a Mrs Margaret Edwardes had a small nursery for babies evacuated from various danger zones, and she went to see what the place was like. She found Mrs Edwardes charming and kindness itself. The house, Yew Lodge, was comfortable and everything was extremely well run. Violette stayed for some weeks with her and bought a pram in which she wheeled Tania through the surrounding country lanes, rich with the scent of summer.

Violette returned to town, greatly worried at not having had a letter from Etienne for some time. She did not know that he had been bottled up in Bir Hakim with the rest of the Foreign Legion. Bir Hakim lay less than fifty miles south-west of Tobruk. General Koenig was in command of the French forces there and British confidence in him and his men was very high. On the night of May 26th–27th, a few days before Tania was born, Rommel, attacking by moonlight, succeeded in encircling this stronghold. Its retention by the Allies was regarded as vital. The French clung on desperately, though attacked incessantly by air and by land. But, after a time, inevitably their supplies began to run out and it became increasingly difficult to replenish them. After a fortnight's most valiant resistance, it had sadly to be decided that Bir Hakim must be evacuated. So once again, as at Narvik, Etienne had to be withdrawn from a position which, despite many sacrifices, could no longer be held. The fierce fighting took a terrible toll. But, hard pressed as they all were, there was no chance of a respite, and the remnants of the Foreign Legion, after being speedily re-grouped, were sent to reinforce the greatly depleted strength of the Eighth Army.

It was not until much later that Violette learned of this. She heard too at last from Etienne. He went into lyrical raptures over the birth of Tania, asked endless questions and poured out his paternal longing to take the child in his arms. That this would be possible soon he still had no doubt, for, despite the critical situation in the desert, he seemed as confident as ever of coming home. 'For Tania's sake, if no other – though I long just as much to be with you – they must, without more delay, grant me this leave – from compassion for a father longing to see his first child.'

But, try hard though he did, Etienne was not able to get leave. Rommel's successes were causing the gravest anxieties. After entering Bir Hakim, he attacked the British forces to the north and turned our flank. There was a culminating tank battle which lasted two days. At its close, as Winston Churchill has recorded, the enemy were masters of the field. Home leave could obviously not be granted in these circumstances. Etienne wrote again to say that in three months perhaps it might be possible for him to be with them. That would make it early in October. More sanguine than that he could not be.

Violette returned to Havant. She decided to bring Tania back with her. The recurrent journeys to Hampshire took too long. She wanted her child nearer at hand. A friend of hers, Miss Maidment, who lived at Mill Hill, had offered to keep the child with her. She was young and gentle, and would undoubtedly look after Tania well. Moreover, Violette could get there quite easily and in no time at all. For herself, her plan was to live in the flat, for it was there that Etienne would be writing to her and that was where he would come, without possibly any warning at all.

The newspapers, however, offered her little hope. She read that the Eighth Army was in retreat again and had been driven back into Egypt. On its heels came Rommel with his Afrika Korps. The situation became increasingly grim. Auchinleck took up a new position 150 miles inside Egypt in the Qattara depression, and soon Rommel thrust at our forces there. So widespread was the general concern that Winston Churchill flew out to Cairo early in August to see for himself what could be done to halt the enemy. The chances of Etienne's home-coming now seemed exceedingly slender. Yet in September Violette heard that leave had been granted. He hoped to be with her early the next month.

Greatly excited, she busied herself in the flat, preparing his welcome. Provisions were bought. She planned to have roses in every room because of his great love of them. And friends were told to be ready for a party the moment Etienne arrived.

But the days passed without further news. A battle was expected almost daily at El Alamein. This was to be

Montgomery's first great thrust and wisely he planned it with the utmost care. It was expected at the end of September, but it had to be deferred. Churchill cabled: "A victorious battle makes amends for much delay." He had to wait nearly a month for the attack, which was launched at last on October 23rd, 1942.

In the opening round of that historic engagement, which marked the turning point of the war in the desert, Etienne was severely wounded. An enemy bullet, fired it may well be by one of the Germans who had served with him in the Foreign Legion and had been allowed by the Vichy Government to join the German Army for this war in the desert, tore into his stomach and it was soon found that the wound was mortal. Etienne died of his injuries twenty-four hours later.

Violette did not learn of this until months afterwards. She waited, meanwhile, still hoping that his leave had merely been delayed by Montgomery's stirring successes, and that one day, quite unexpectedly, she would find him on the doorstep. She continued to write to him. Her letters were wholly about the child, the progress Tania was making, her first smile, so radiantly lovely, her halting efforts to say "Da Da". She waited for his answers, but of course none came.

Living alone, she wandered often amid the scenes of her own childhood in Bayswater, revisiting the familiar streets, seeing again at every turning little sights that had once delighted her. But the old watchman, with a red lamp outside his shelter, was no longer there to offer her one of the sausages he was cooking for his supper, and, in the rows of houses around, the bombs had torn many gaps.

As the weeks passed she began to have doubts, wondering if he was wounded, if by some awful mischance something worse might have happened. She could no longer bear to be alone. She locked up the fiat and went back to Brixton to live with her parents. Again and again she called in person at the Free French headquarters in Carlton Gardens to ask for news of Etienne. But they had none, no news at all of him. "We have your address. We shall write," they said, "the moment we hear."

At her father's urging, so as to take her mind off things, she agreed to go to the aircraft factory at Morden where he was working. They were glad of the extra help. She applied herself earnestly, though her mind was in a turbulence of uncertainty. The one encouraging thought, indeed assurance, for her was that he must have been taken prisoner, for that usually was when one did not hear. In the general confusion caused by Montgomery's magnificent advances, little could be known about prisoners. She clung to that one hope but, pursuing it by her inquiries at the Red Cross and elsewhere, she was able to learn nothing.

That, despite the doubts and misgivings that agitated her mind, she did her work well at the factory is supported by the evidence of those who worked with her. In no time at all she was put in charge of a section. At home, however, her father and mother were only too aware of her listlessness and her despondency. "If anything has happened to Etienne," Mrs Bushell told her husband, "it will be terrible for her."

The news came at last and its effect was shattering. Violette was unable to go on with her work and stayed at home in utter dejection for some days. Then quite suddenly she announced to her father: "I'm leaving the factory. I want to do more – much more in this war." Surely there was some way – she felt there must be. She wanted to fight with a gun in her hand – and the women's services did not let you do that.

What had she in mind, her parents wondered? For some weeks they were aware only of her restlessness. She went up to London day after day, came back late in the evening, when she came back at all. She was entirely uncommunicative as to what she was doing or trying to do.

"She'll settle down," said Mrs Bushell, trying as always to look at the pleasanter side. But Mr Bushell was not at all sure. He feared that, reacting to the shock, she had gone to the other extreme and was abandoning herself to a life of diversion – the theatre, dancing in the evenings, out till the dawn in night clubs. He didn't like it. He didn't like it at all.

Chapter 8

The Interview

There is no doubt that the shattering news about Etienne threatened to affect her outlook and her entire future. But she was not left to her sombre and melancholy reveries for long. A week or so later she received a brief and baffling letter signed 'E. Potter', a name she had never heard before. It invited her to come to an address in Sanctuary Buildings, Westminster.

She said nothing of the letter to her parents, although it was at their home in Brixton that it had arrived for her. On the appointed day, inquiring her way, she went to Great Smith Street, and found Sanctuary Buildings, a massive and hideous nine-story block of grey stone, not far from Westminster Abbey. She entered No 3, as directed in the letter, and was met in the spacious front hall by a man wearing the ordinary uniform of a commissionaire. There was nothing to suggest that the place had any link at all with the war, except perhaps in its aftermath, since it seemed to be chiefly used for housing the Ministry of Pensions.

Violette asked for Room 531 and, after filling in a form on which she had to state her name and address, she was taken up by an attendant. Here she saw, seated at a table, a slightly-built gentleman in his early forties, wearing a quiet lounge suit. The room was starkly functional, for it was furnished, in spite of its size, with one plain deal table and two equally plain chairs and absolutely nothing else. The dingy cream walls were quite bare except for a large notice dealing with Air Raid Precautions; the windows were boarded up, either because they had been blown out or in expectation of being blown out. So the light came from one bright, naked electric light bulb in mid–ceiling.

Potter stood up, greeted her in a friendly, relaxed way, gave her the visitor's chair and sat down again behind the table. She still could not see anything about him or the room to suggest that his interest was connected in any way with promoting the war effort or that his work could be valuable or at all strenuous. Her anticipations accordingly dwindled.

But Potter was in fact concerned with the war in a very close and intimate way. He was not actually Potter at all, but Captain Selwyn Jepson, of the Buffs. Before the war he was a successful writer of mystery stories and the son of an equally distinguished writer, Edgar Jepson. Several of his books had already been filmed and later others were to be adapted for the screen by that mystifier Alfred Hitchcock. But he was not sitting in this uncomfortable room to discuss mystery stories, although one might say he was here to cause other people to live them. He had been seconded from the Directorate of Military Intelligence to an organisation as secret as the work it did.

It was his particular job to find secret agents. He had scouts on the lookout, but even they did not know for what purpose he wanted men and women with a knowledge of France and fluency in speaking French. From the Admiralty, the War Office, the Air Ministry, from the Central Bureau of Registration at the Ministry of Labour and National Service, and other less official sources, names were forwarded to him. In this instance he had heard of Violette from his liaison with the War Office. He had asked in the usual way if she might be sent up from her ATS unit for an interview, but had been somewhat taken aback by the reply. He was informed that, since her name had been passed on to him, she had been discharged from the ATS on compassionate grounds. Compassionate grounds? Security forbade his asking what these were, since that kind of curiosity from him might interest the ATS branch in his activities – and he did not want that. It could of course mean that there was something wrong with her health, or that she had been urgently required to help at home because of someone there who was ill and dependent on her. Actually her own physical fitness was absolutely essential, since the work for which she was required would be both tough and dangerous. However, his need being great at the time, he wrote to her at her home, a letter of sufficient vagueness to conceal its ultimate purpose.

He had two addresses at which he interviewed such candidates – this one at the Ministry of Pensions in Sanctuary Buildings and the second, a room at the Victoria Hotel in Northumberland Avenue, then occupied largely by the Quartermaster-General's directorate. There was a third address, a flat in Orchard Court, the large modern block in Portman Square, but this was not used for interviews, only for seeing agents who had already been selected and were about to begin their training; and every precaution was taken so that they should not meet those secret agents who had just returned from operations abroad.

This secret organisation had been set up very soon after the fall of France. In that grim summer of 1940, while many in Britain saw in the sad fate of the great French nation nothing but a fulfilment of their fear that the French could not really be relied on, there were others who regarded that judgment as unjust and severe. In their view, it was not faintheartedness or cowardice that had made the French Army crumble, but lack of tanks and aircraft to stem the formidable onrush of the German panzer divisions. They foresaw rightly that the people of France, who are intractable and unruly when driven, could not live tamely under the iron heel of Nazism, however masked by a show of correctness. This was soon confirmed. Of the British soldiers taken prisoner at St Valery, some managed to escape and were greatly assisted in their journey across enemy-occupied France by the French people. They were given clothes, food, shelter, and even money. Again and again the people of France displayed their readiness to risk their lives in order to aid the cause of Allied victory. It was even more abundantly confirmed by the incessant flow to Britain of French refugees who were eager to carry on the fight under General de Gaulle. They reported that small groups were springing up in various parts of occupied France, resolved on resisting the enemy by whatever means they could. Some pounced on German sentries in the dark and slit their throats, for which many who were innocent paid with their lives in the heavy retribution exacted by the Germans.

It was with Churchill's famous directive to 'Set Europe in flames' that the work began of encouraging the many Resistance movements which were springing up all over Europe in the wake of the German advance. These movements, if haphazard and unco-ordinated, if left without arms and equipment, would have achieved only self-destruction. So an organisation was created in London to assist them. It was nominally under the Minister of Economic Warfare, but was answerable to its own Chief of Staff. Norway, Holland, Belgium, Yugoslavia, Italy and Greece each had their own section, but of them all France was by far the largest and most promising for such operations. Recruitment had necessarily to be conducted with the greatest care, since German spies were obviously infiltrating with the crowds of refugees from France.

General de Gaulle's Free French organisation also began to function in the same way but on a more limited scale. The two, however, were kept apart for security reasons, and only rarely had direct contact with each other or engaged in mutual activities. Yeo-Thomas, who was known as 'The White Rabbit', was exceptional in having first served with the Free French.

The French Section of the British organisation – its full title: 'Special Operations Executive' or SOE – was formed in February 1941 and came under the control of Captain Maurice Buckmaster. Buckmaster had before the war been working for the Ford Motor Company in Europe. He knew France well and was admirably suited for the work he was about to undertake. He had gone with the British Expeditionary Force to France as Intelligence Officer, had been evacuated at Dunkirk, and was about to return to France, for our army was still fighting at St Valery, when he was sent with the de Gaulle expedition to Dakar in French West Africa. The plan was to rally the African possessions of France under the flag of freedom. But a leakage led to the Germans informing Pétain of it and arranging for him to resist de Gaulle's landing. Following an unfortunate scuffle outside Dakar, de Gaulle went on to French Equatorial Africa and established himself there. Buckmaster returned to England.

A few days after Buckmaster came to the French Section he was joined by Miss Vera Atkins, who also knew France exceedingly well. She kept in close and constant touch with the agents from the moment of their recruitment, throughout their period of training and even after their dispatch to France.

The earliest recruits were soon under training, each with his *nom de guerre,* and in the course of three months went from one specialised course to another until they were ready for 'the field'. They were sent to France in fishing boats, landed by submarine, or dropped by parachute. At first they had no reception committees to meet them but had to pick up such threads as they could, and they faced, of course, very grave dangers, not only from the vigilant Germans, but also from many French people, who were constantly being roused by the Vichy Government against Britain's attempts to bring the French Navy, and overseas dominions in Africa and elsewhere, into de Gaulle's fold. There was indeed a great deal of bitter feeling in France over the incident at Oran, where, to prevent some of the finest French battleships from falling into German hands, a British naval force went to beg them to join us. When this was refused, our warships opened fire to deny them to the enemy. A heavy engagement followed, in the course of which the French battleship *Bretagne* was blown up, the *Dunquerque* ran aground, and the *Provence* was beached by its crew. So great was the wrath of Pétain over this that in retaliation he ordered the bombing of Gibraltar. Many in France were sadly bewildered. They could not imagine what they had done to deserve these fresh misfortunes at the hands of their recent ally. Fortunately these doubts were not generally prevalent. The majority of the people in France were clear in their purpose, which was to free their country from the Nazi oppressors. The earliest of our secret agents found sixty per cent of the people well disposed towards the Allied cause, quite a large number of these were in fact prepared to help us. Only about twenty per cent were decidedly hostile, a large enough number, amounting in all to many scattered millions. The remainder were anxious only to keep clear of trouble and would not take sides one way or the other, fearful not only of life or liberty, but of the confiscation of their possessions.

Moving with caution, our agents managed to weld the scattered and unorganised resisters into small effective groups. Each group, or circuit as it was called, needed a leader and as a rule the agent, trained to do so, took on that role himself. It needed also as an essential a small portable wireless transmitting set in order to keep in touch with the headquarters in London. Radio operators were already being trained in England for such work and small portable transmitting sets were being specially made for this purpose. Specified times were arranged for the transmission, generally twice a day. They were in code, of course. The voice was not used; the signals were in Morse. In London a group of operators, similarly trained, received these vital messages, giving information of inestimable value about war factories and railways and troop movements, and were sent in return clear directions for various forms of sabotage, which became in time a grave and baffling problem for the occupying Germans.

Our earliest agents, landing without any contacts at all, had to grope their way carefully. Several were caught and tortured by the Gestapo, who sought to wrest from them the secrets of their underground work. But those who escaped detection laid the foundations of a vast network that was in time to cover all France and was of the utmost importance in the conduct of the war. They greatly aided the Allied armies of liberation after the landings on D-Day, as will be seen.

The earliest agents had to make their own way back to England as best they could, coming across the Pyrenees and Spain or being picked up at night by a submarine or a fishing boat, if somehow or other they had been able to get a message home. But as each circuit was formed a more direct contact was established. Our agents landed by parachute on selected fields provided by sympathetic farmers. Reception committees were formed to guide the drops with prearranged light signals and, where the field was large enough and conditions favourable, it was sometimes possible to land a plane. Small Lysanders, able to fly slowly at low altitudes, were used for this purpose, and were guided in on a short wave signalling call. An almost regular ferry service was in time established in this way. Many French men and women, scientists needed for war work, and others being hunted by the Gestapo, were contacted by our agents and brought to England in the returning planes. It was a Scarlet Pimpernel service on swift up-to-date lines.

The Germans knew of course what was afoot. They had detector vans constantly on the prowl to locate the radio transmitters, catch the operators and learn from them by every means they could employ the time and place of these landings. Some operators were caught, others had to go into hiding for a time. And the landing-places had constantly to be changed.

As the field of operations widened it became obvious that more and more agents and wireless operators would be required; and it was eventually decided to recruit girls for such work. Vera Atkins says there were heated discussions when this was first suggested. But women were in fact ideally suitable, especially for such jobs as wireless operators and couriers, since they were likely to attract less attention in enemy-occupied country than men, of whom there were naturally very few about at the time: millions were prisoners of war in Germany, and, as those remaining had known jobs on farms or in factories, new faces in any area were all too noticeable.

The recruitment of women as secret agents began in the spring of 1942, just a year before Selwyn Jepson, as E. Potter, wrote to ask Violette to come and see him in Sanctuary Buildings. Sitting behind his bare table, with a single sheet of paper before him on which he pencilled an occasional note, he began his exploration in a quiet, gentle voice.

He says Violette looked older than the twenty-two years she gave as her age; she had a certain maturity of poise and expression that made her seem twenty-six or seven. She seemed healthy, even strong, and he soon brought her to the subject of her release from the ATS on compassionate grounds. He asked if she felt quite well again.

"Yes," she said, "thank you."

"Was it anything serious?"

"No," she replied, thinking of the near-to-breakdown stage she had recently reached on learning of Etienne's death.

"May I ask what was the matter?"

"My husband was killed at El Alamein. I'm afraid I took it rather badly."

This surprised him. He had been given to understand she was *Miss* Szabo.

"Were you married long?"

"No. In fact we were together for only a very few weeks."

"I'm sorry. How very sad … and now you're living with your parents?"

"Yes."

He went on to ask her about her life before the war and gradually learned more and more about her. He felt that her qualifications were excellent for the work he had in mind.

Then she asked a question. "What did you want me for?"

"I was thinking your knowledge of France and your fluency in French might be very useful."

"In what way?"

"Well," he said, "it comes under the heading of dangerous work."

She received this with the momentary silence to which he was accustomed. They generally guessed now, or came very near it.

"You mean – spying?" she asked.

"No. This is different, but in some ways the conditions are similar. It calls for special training as well as special qualifications, and, after that, it means moving about, living, and doing this particular job, in enemy-occupied territory."

"In France?"

"In France, where we are trying to make things as unpleasant and difficult for the Germans as we can. Sabotage in fact – from blowing up their troop trains and immobilising their commandeered factories to putting chalk in their ink." His eyes were serious in spite of the light note at the end. "And," he said, "they don't like it. They react violently and brutally."

He knew what he was talking about and so did she, now.

"That would suit me very well," she said without hesitation.

This bothered him. Immediate, unqualified, unquestioning acceptance was always disappointing. And yet there was nothing casual or irresponsible about her that he could detect.

"It would? Why?"

She thought, but only for a short moment, and said slowly:

"I wouldn't mind dying the way he died."

This worried him even more. It sounded too much like self-immolation, not a motive to encourage and certainly not one in which to involve other people. An agent in these better organised days worked seldom on his own.

"That seems to put rather an emphasis on dying," he said. "We want our people to live, not die. To live and fight the war. So you see how difficult it would be to have anyone around who saw a situation as a possible means of rejoining someone she had lost through death."

"I did not mean that," she said. "You mentioned danger. I only wanted to make it clear that I am prepared to face danger – of that kind. It is true I have felt since my husband's death that I have little to live for. But if the work you give me is worth while in the sort of way his was, as a soldier, I shall have a great deal to live for, and if it ends as it ended for him – well, that's all right too."

There were times when the burden of this job he was doing was heavier than at others, and this was one of them. Humanly, he could have wished her less good-looking. She was too pretty altogether to talk of death, let alone consider it.

But he had to be reassured, and was. The clarity no less than the quickness of her analysis showed it was genuine. He felt she would make a good agent, even a very good one, if all went well.

He asked her the next question. Had she anybody dependent on her?

She hesitated a moment. "Both my parents are alive," she said. But not a word came from her about her child. Had Jepson known that afternoon, he feels now, looking back on it, that he would have stopped the conversation there. "The loss of her husband outweighed everything, even her motherhood – desperation which I should have seen as weakness. But, as it turned out, she derived strength from her training and from integration with the small group of men and women with whom she was trained for the work. Indeed she reacted in this way to a remarkable degree and the death-wish business (which after all was in the comparative safety of her consciousness and not buried somewhere deep inside her) completely cleared up, and that was all I was really worried about.

"In the same way, as her preparation progressed, she was carried over the apparent indifference to the child by a true dedication to what she had chosen to do. It was bigger than she was, bigger than anything else. The self-immolation prospect disappeared. I am sure of that. If it came back it would have been only at the end, when it would have been a comfort and a strength. Nothing less."

But he did not know about the child until much later, by which time she had so convinced everyone of her enthusiasm and capabilities that no one could have been deterred from letting her go through with it. "Violette gave us all the belief that she would be successful."

He ended this first interview with her by saying: "I'd like you to think this over very seriously indeed, and let me know in about a week whether it's the sort of thing you want to undertake. I don't have to tell you that you must think all this over alone. The security on this is absolute."

"I don't need to think it over," she said. "I know it's what I want to do. I can tell you that now."

"Well, I'd like to think it over myself," he replied. "I'll write to you in about a week's time." His intention was in any case to obtain a full clearance on her from MI5 before he went any further.

He got up and held out his hand.

"May I," she asked, "have your telephone number?"

He gave her the general number of the Ministry of Pensions, and first thing the next morning she used it, the call being re-routed through at least three switchboards to his line at the Baker Street headquarters of the French Section of SOE.

"Have you decided?" she asked.

"Not yet," he replied. "As I told you, I'll let you know in about a week."

The call indicated her eagerness, but he knew of that already. He hoped all the same that it would not prevent her thinking it over seriously; he did not want her to have second thoughts against it, but he wanted her to have second thoughts before her final decision was made. His problem was that there were very few as qualified as she was among the many who passed through his net.

A week or so later, having received the all clear from MI5, he wrote to her from No. 3 Sanctuary Buildings, in order not as yet to reveal any other address, and he still used his cover-name of Potter. A second interview was arranged at which he indicated that, although she obviously could not serve in France in uniform, it was important under international law that she should be given a Service position of some kind. He explained that in due course she would have to be enrolled as an officer in the First Aid Nursing Yeomanry, familiarly known as FANY. This was an independent voluntary corps of women, formed in 1907, the year the Territorials came into being: in that year women were also able for the first time to become aldermen and mayors. Those anxious to serve in this new corps were given instruction in First Aid and in riding. It was primarily regarded as an adjunct to the ambulance service and women were expected to go into the fighting line on horseback and bring back the wounded to the ambulance stations. They rendered admirable service during the First World War. Many displayed the greatest bravery under fire and won a number of decorations. Since 1939 the FANYs had been running motor ambulance units in Finland and in France; they also drove ambulances for the Red Cross, served in Forces canteens in

Britain, and acted as chauffeurs for officers of the British
Army. At the prospect of invasion in 1940 many were put on to
packing explosives for the Home Guard or for dispatch to the
underground forces in occupied Europe. To this extent their
work was closely allied to the work Violette was now called
upon to do. SOE was served by a Motor Transport Section of
this service, and the machinery for enlisting the women agents
into it was already in existence. It provided an excellent cover
for them while they were training in Britain – and, when the
time came for them to go into the field, it was still useful, since
the FANYs were known to be serving in all the theatres of the
war abroad and in none of the other women's services,
recognised by the Army Act, was it permitted for women to
carry weapons. So in due course Violette was commissioned as
an officer in the FANYs. She was made a subaltern and wore
one red 'raspberry' on her shoulder-straps.

Her parents meanwhile, completely unaware of these
developments, could hardly be blamed for wondering why
Violette was doing nothing after saying she wanted to take a
more active part in the war. To them, though several weeks had
gone by since she left the aircraft factory at Morden, she still
appeared to be doing nothing at all. And in fact for some weeks,
until she was finally accepted, she had been doing nothing.
Since the news of Etienne's death, she had been living only on
the small pension paid by the Free French. Out of this she had
her child's keep at Mill Hill to pay for and there wasn't enough
over for the rent of her flat and her own living expenses. Again
and again she debated whether she should not give up the flat
and go back to her parents, but, if the appointment came, the
flat she felt would be a useful centre. The financial strain,
meanwhile, was great. She was aware that, with the acute
shortage of labour, it would be easy to find work at a more
ample remuneration than she could hope to get for the
dangerous work she was to undertake. But she preferred to
wait, and eased the strain by taking on odd jobs, such as
helping out for a few hours in a shop and being a
photographer's model. The one thing she was determined not
to do was to miss the opportunity of becoming a secret agent.

C.N.P   F

70

So she waited. Her cigarettes she always got for nothing at the shooting gallery at Marble Arch where she had won them so often before.

Then at last came the appointment and she went down to Brixton in her new uniform. She looked very smart and everyone assumed that she would now be happy, having obviously found the more useful and active war work she wanted. But just how useful and active she was to be only she and a handful of people knew.

Chapter 9

Initial Training

Early in September Violette arrived at Sanctuary Buildings for her third interview and was taken by Jepson to Orchard Court in Portman Square. There in a four-roomed flat, which had been in private occupation before the war and was now sparsely furnished with a table and a few chairs in each room, various discussions seemed to be in progress. Some were busily talking in the kitchen, others in the bathroom. A group of about a dozen, about to embark on their initial training as secret agents, waited in what was once the drawing-room. They were all in uniform, the girls dressed as FANYs, the men in the uniform of some corps to which they were nominally attached. It was at this stage that Jepson introduced Violette to Buckmaster and to Vera Atkins, who had walked down the short distance of a hundred yards or so from the headquarters of SOE in Baker Street. There was a short impersonal talk on the aims of the organisation and the purpose of the training. Then each was allotted a distinctive Christian name by which he or she was to be known at the first school. That name would be changed as they progressed to further courses. This was done in order to make it difficult for other agents or unauthorised people to keep track of any individual members from one stage to the next. Violette, in the course of her training and her work, had in all six different names – Louise, Reine, Corinne and so on – but for the purpose of consistency and clarity she is called Violette throughout this narrative.

The talk over, the group, accompanied by two escorting officers, one for the girls, of whom there were only four, and the other for the men, set out by coach for Wanborough Manor, an attractive old country house standing in a very large garden a few miles outside Guildford. The nearest village was quaintly, and in Violette's case significantly, called Normandy.

Here they were received by Major Roger de Wesselow, tall, elegant, every inch a Guards officer, who was before the war head of an organisation connected with books on form in horse-racing. The new batch had the place to themselves. There was no overlapping with pupils from a previous group, for every month saw a fresh course begin. There was one training officer, two NCOs to assist him and the two escorting officers who kept the trainees under friendly but searching scrutiny and reported constantly to Jepson who was responsible for weeding out any who were unlikely to prove suitable. Everything mattered: all the personal idiosyncrasies, aptitudes or lack of them; temperamental reaction to their companions, to strain and tension, to success and to disappointment.

The house had large bedrooms, which they shared four or five to a room. The beds were most comfortable. The food, which was supervised by a French cook, was exceptionally good and plentiful. They were allowed special rations and the larder was stacked with a variety of good things not normally available at the time. As de Wesselow says, it was in some ways a drawing-room life. The aim was to put them all completely at their ease and in a relaxed mood, so that, at this early stage, many would be seen off their guard and much might be learned of their true spirit and outlook.

Violette and some of the others, despite what Jepson had said, were convinced in their own minds that they were about to become spies. But in fact, beyond the assumption of an alias and later the evolution of a new identity, with their normal backgrounds completely obliterated, there was nothing in the training approximating even remotely to any preconceived ideas one had of Olga Polowsky and other famous spies of song or story. To that extent it must have been disillusioning to some. They were told, of course, that on their behaviour and circumspection would depend not only the success of the operation they were to be sent out to undertake, but even the lives of their comrades. One had therefore to be secretive without being suspected and this undoubtedly offered some solace as being a little along the lines expected.

De Wesselow, assembling them, indicated that there would be lectures as well as both practical and physical training. They were taught map-reading, signalling in the Morse code, the handling of weapons, such as revolvers, rifles and hand grenades, a knowledge of explosives and their most effective application for purposes of sabotage, and they were put through the initial stages of parachute jumping, confined here chiefly to the art of falling without hurting oneself, a technique derived largely from the comedians of Fred Karno. Physically they had the usual jerks and drills – just the preliminary stages of toughening to test how much each was able to endure. They had to rise early in the morning and run before breakfast across the fields to the top of the Hog's Back. The more strenuous exercises included all-in wrestling, which brought a mass of aches and bruises. They played tennis and swam in the private pool among the pine trees. The evenings were diversified with indoor games designed to sharpen their sense of perception. They were given a quick glimpse of a tray littered with a variety of articles and had to enumerate afterwards what these were. This was followed by charades. Conversation at all times and particularly during meals had to be in French. All letters received and sent out were censored. The use of the telephone was absolutely barred.

At the end of the month, the course having been completed, all the candidates returned to their homes. Meanwhile at headquarters the reports on them were scrutinised and in those cases where there was still a doubt the candidate was discarded. Few indeed survived their first stage of training and inspection. Only the most alert, the most composed and the most resourceful were allowed to go on. Violette was overjoyed when, a fortnight later, she was informed that she was one of the few selected.

She spent part of her time off in her flat in Pembridge Villas. Almost daily she went to see her child at Mill Hill.

Occasionally she spent a night with her parents in Brixton. Here endless questions were asked her. Being in uniform she was able to answer some of them. Dad was vaguely aware of the FANYs in the First World War. Not unnaturally he wanted to know what exactly Violette was doing. She explained that she helped in a Forces canteen for the most part, but from time to time had to drive a lorry to Nottingham or Bristol, taking stores – and that of course took her out of town for days on end.

"That what you've been doing for the past month?" he asked.

"Yes," she said, a little uncomfortably. She wondered if it sounded like a lie, for she had never before had to evade their questioning.

Dad looked at her doubtfully.

"I see," he said, "and I suppose you'll be off again presently?"

"Yes," she replied. "In about a week from now."

"And where's this canteen of yours?" He obviously had very grave doubts.

"Oh, at different places – Ealing – West Kensington – Birmingham. I have to go and lend a hand all over the place."

"I see." But it was clear that he didn't. In order to avoid further questioning, and also from a desire to see something of the others who were in the same service, Violette decided to live for the most part in town. Her flat was central enough and quite easily accessible. Almost every evening friends dropped in for a drink and a chat. They played the gramophone and danced, or they went out together for a meal to the Studio Club, across the Park in Knightsbridge. Occasionally in a party of four or six they went on to a night club, where they danced to popular rhythms of the time, including the one which was her favourite and was asked for again and again, *I'll Be Around*. She had a record of it, made by the Mills Brothers, and often played it, all raising their voices as they joined in the chorus.

The second and far more strenuous stage of the training was in Scotland. The train journey was long and tedious. They had to change at Glasgow, go on in a small train to a little station near Mallaig, transfer to a lorry and drive the rest of the way along narrow, winding, bumpy lanes to a small country house at Arisaig on the Inverness coast which was to be their home for the next month or so.

Here they were put through the entire commando course. There was no let-up for the girls, they too had to do it all. For many miles around them were other training centres at which similar courses were being conducted for Norwegians, Poles, Dutch, Belgians and others training either to be secret agents or uniformed commandos. These groups were kept apart, of course.

The area was big enough to ensure this: the west coast of Scotland was sparsely populated and ideally cut off from the world; and the same instructors were shared with the minimum of travel. Amongst these were experts of all kinds – rock-climbers, explorers, big-game hunters, canoeists and judo experts.

It was a most strenuous, indeed a drastic course of training. Everything was stepped up. There was regular practice now with not only revolvers and rifles, but with Sten guns, Tommy guns and machineguns, as well as a variety of French and German weapons in case these were all that came to hand in enemy territory, after possibly pouncing on a German and killing him. They used hand grenades and bombs too and a wide range of explosives during their exercises in sabotage. They learned to gauge the charge needed for blowing up a bridge, which varied of course according to the size of the bridge, as well as the more delicate ways of dealing with vital parts of machinery in a factory. During these exercises the air resounded with bangs all day long for miles around. They were taught canoeing and had to lay heavy charges at the bottom of the sea linked with electric wires to a detonator on land. A great diversity of most ingenious booby-traps had also to be circumvented.

They had to set out on long treks across the mountains, travelling often twenty-five miles in bitter weather, mist or rain, guided only by compass. Some got lost in the mountains and had to be rescued. They had to scale almost impossible cliffs, at first by day, then in dark glasses, and eventually by night, always burdened with heavy coils of wire, a load of explosives, hand grenades and guns. They had to wade across ice-cold rivers at two o'clock in the morning, sleep under the stars, however severe the night, and on a hill-top without blankets in the pouring rain. They had to climb walls and leap across from one roof-top to the next by day as well as by night. They had to shin up ropes and drainpipes, break open doors of houses, blow out the front of safes. Progressively the training became more and more arduous until in the end they were sent on raids in which live ammunition was used. This was done to force them to utilise the best possible cover. As though all this was not enough, many diverted themselves in the evenings by forming raiding-parties of their own and trekked for miles across difficult country in the dark to relieve some other training camp of its gin and whisky.

Violette's conducting officer Peggy Minchin, who is now Mrs Turbett, remembers two things in particular about this period of her training. "One is how good she was at weapon training. She had the eye of a hawk and was very quickly extremely efficient with both automatic and Sten gun. I commented on this to her one day and she said: 'I only want to have some Germans to fight and I should die happy if I could take some of them with me.' She seemed quite determined to fight – she was always very single-minded about it.

"She used to entertain us, when we were doing our physical training, by literally tying herself into knots with acrobatic turns. But the other thing I especially remember about her training in Scotland was when two ropes were slung between trees about twenty feet from the ground. You had to place your feet on the bottom rope and hold on to the top one as you walked across from one tree to the other. I could never pluck up courage to try it. But it was just Violette's cup of tea. She would set out quite briskly along the rope, stop halfway and indulge in idle banter with the chaps below, while she swayed dangerously in the breeze, holding on by one hand and her toes.

"Though essentially feminine, there was something gallant, debonair and quite genuine about her. I shall never forget how gaily she crawled through bog and burns and heather during her field training and flung herself over the most hair-raising obstacles in our private assault course, being almost eaten alive by midges all the time."

Special instruction was given by the gamekeeper to His Majesty King George VI on how to take cover in open country, how to stalk and how to avoid being stalked, and, equally important, how to live off the land if one happened to be on the run. They learned how to catch rabbits and pigeons, how to strip the animals and prepare them for eating; what berries were edible and which should be avoided because they were poisonous.

In the final stage of this course each one in turn had to take charge of an operation in order to show his or her ingenuity and initiative in leadership. It was obvious that there would be a further weeding out. Violette, who had the good fortune to be brought up with nearly a dozen brothers and male cousins, was exceedingly efficient, and her admirable state of health enabled her to stand up to the great strain. She emerged in consequence from the course a fully-fledged female commando.

The next stage in her training was at the Parachute School at Ringway, a few miles south of Manchester.

The preliminaries here, before one actually attempted to jump out of a plane with a parachute, were further exercises in falling. One learned to fall with both legs kept close together and to roll over to the right or the left with both hands in the pockets. Falls of every kind were practised over and over again. There followed a series of exercises with the parachute harness strapped on, culminating in jumps from a lofty gallery in the hanger. The parachute itself was not used at this stage, control of the fall was maintained by a cable. It was almost a trapeze act, with the added complication of having to handle the harness. And so progressively until one jumped with a parachute first from a tower and then from a platform attached to a barrage balloon at a height of nearly 900 feet.

At last came the final phase, the drop from an aircraft. Whitley bombers were used for this. Few escaped the feeling of uneasiness, and even fear, as the doors opened and one dropped through space, wondering all the while whether the parachute would open and one would land safely. For all these tests a static line was employed. It was a length of cable attached to the parachute on your back, which tugged the 'chute open automatically and did not leave its manipulation to your fumbling nervousness.

Violette had to make five such jumps from the plane and was apparently not in the least bit nervous. But on her second fall, as she reached the earth, despite all her care in rolling over, her ankle got twisted and was badly sprained. One could see as she rose after unstrapping the harness that she was walking with a marked limp. The ankle was swelling rapidly and all further jumps were thereupon cancelled. She was sent home for rest and treatment.

She travelled down by train, her left foot in bandages, and went to Brixton to stay with her parents, whom she had not seen for more than two months. Their welcome was eager. Concerned inquiries were made about her ankle. But, from Papa especially, there was a questioning also about her long absence. He asked where she had been and what she had been doing. The only address they had was a box number at the post office in Wimpole Street. Her letters to them, postmarked West London, were brief and revealed nothing.

Once again she had to be evasive. She trotted out the old stuff about working in canteens and driving lorries and could see that it was not going down at all well. It made her embarrassed and self-conscious. It was not easy to lie to those one loved, and she hoped most fervently that it would not be so difficult when she was questioned by the enemy, towards whom of course her feelings would be violently different. After a time Papa abandoned his efforts. But, when dinner was over, he sat alone with her in the lounge and said he wanted to have a talk with her.

"I don't know what you get up to," he began, "but I know you are very pretty and that men have always been interested in you. Now don't tell me that you're grown up, that you've been married and have a child. That does not qualify you to do what you like. You should realise that it is very natural for parents to be concerned, especially in times like this. Your mother and I have had many sleepless nights wondering what you might be up to."

"Oh, Dad! How absurd! I'm not the first girl to join the Forces."

"I know that. And do you think what you're doing – canteen work, driving lorries, driving cars for generals and what not – is more useful – is helping to win the war – more, for instance, than your work in the aircraft factory?"

" I do," she said.

"Well, I don't," he countered with some emphasis. "And what about your time off? What do you do with that? You meet men, don't you?"

"I'm with men all the time, Dad. It's part of my work. There's nothing wrong in that."

"Don't you go dancing any more?"

"Yes – when I can. We danced at the ack–ack battery, you already know about that – and we dance sometimes in the canteen after the tables have been cleared."

"And what about the officers? Do you go about with them?"

"Why, of course. I'm an officer myself now. We sometimes go in a party to the theatre and go on afterwards to a night club. There's no harm in that, surely."

"There could be. Look, Vi. I wish you'd live at home with us. Your mother and I would like that – instead of you rushing about all over the place."

"I can't. I've got to get about – it's part of my work."

"And get your foot into that ghastly state? Is that helping to win the war too?" He was getting quite worked up now.

"I told you. I twisted it jumping out of a lorry."

"You expect me to believe that?"

"Why are you so suspicious, Dad? What does the twisted ankle prove – that I've been having a mad flirtation with a colonel?"

"I don't know what to think."

"Oh, don't be so absurd. And please don't go on about it," she said. "I'm most dreadfully tired." She was about to rise.

"All right! All right!" he said finally, raising his voice. "You do what you like. But I tell you this. If you're not careful, my girl, you'll come to a bad end. You mark my words."

Her lips tightened slightly, but her face was like a mask. She leaned forward to pick up her handbag. With her thoughts elsewhere, she clasped it insecurely and, as it fell forward, it opened and almost everything in it was scattered about the floor.

Her father was too angry to help her pick anything up. So she got down on all fours herself and, moving carefully with her bandaged foot, retrieved her lipstick, the compact, her purse, which had opened out too, and she had to stretch for the coins that had rolled far away. Her father, relenting a little now, helped her to pick up the last few things.

She shut her bag, rose and, with a weary 'Good night', limped out of the room.

After she had gone he sat sucking at his pipe for a long time, wondering about her. There was nothing more he could say – or do for that matter. After all she was old enough: she was twenty-two – a widow – and a mother.

Mrs Bushell, having said good night to her at the foot of the stairs just as Violette was limping up to her bedroom, came in and sat with Mr Bushell, and they talked for well over an hour about her evasions and her vague excuses until they too, feeling tired, got up to go to bed.

As he moved towards the door of the sitting-room Mr Bushell noticed something lying on the floor, half hidden by the sofa. He drew it out and was startled to see that it was a parachute badge. He held it out in his hand towards his wife and tears began to course down his cheeks. Everything suddenly became quite clear. He could hardly speak, and when he did his words came with difficulty through his sobs. He had suspected the girl, challenged her cruelly. He had used many harsh, hurtful words – and all the while, with neither reproach nor rebuke, Violette had suffered it, without betraying her secret.

Mr and Mrs Bushell passed the badge from one to the other, wept a little, and were very proud of their daughter – and yet they could not understand what canteens and lorries or even First Aid, the normal work of the FANYs, had to do with jumping out of a plane by parachute.

"She'll tell us when she can," said Mrs Bushell, and, taking her husband's hand in hers, they walked together through a mist to their room.

At breakfast the next morning her father said, "How do you like parachuting, Vi?"

She flushed. "How did you know, Dad?"

He held out the badge.

"Thanks."

"It fell out of your bag."

They ate in silence for a while, then, unable to resist it, Mr Bushell asked: "Have you to do much more of it?"

Looking him full in the eye, all her evasions now behind her, Violette sighed with relief. "I can't tell you anything. I'm not allowed to, Dad. I'm under oath."

"OK, Vi," he said. "I can guess what the job is. I won't ask you any more questions."

And he never did.

Chapter 10

Finishing School

The injured ankle caused a break of more than a month in Violette's training. A doctor had examined it at Ringway and treated it; now a local doctor, to whom nothing could of course be revealed of the cause, came in from time to time to see it. When it was pronounced to be definitely on the mend, Violette went off to Bournemouth to convalesce. There, on the doctor's insistence that the foot should be given a complete rest, she went about in a bath chair as so many of the residents there do, but, since a span of half a century separated her age from theirs, many looked and wondered, glanced down sympathetically at the bandages and asked about the bombing in London, which seemed to them to be the cause of the injury. She kept up the fiction and adhered rigidly to the treatment, for it was her resolve to get fit as quickly as possible in order to resume the courses, at the end of which she would have of course to go back to Ringway for the rest of her jumps.

Late in November 1943, her foot being at last out of bandages, she went on to Beaulieu in the New Forest in Hampshire for her final training at what had come to be called the finishing school. The headquarters of this establishment, where the staff of instructors were housed, was in the home of Lord Montagu of Beaulieu, who was at the time only sixteen years old. He was away most of the year at Eton and came home only for the school holidays. The candidates were spread out in various country houses for many miles around, about twenty minutes or so by car from each other and often even further from Beaulieu. The houses stood in their own parks, some of them enormously large, and had been taken over from their private owners. The grouping was by nationality. To one house were assigned the Polish trainees, to another the Dutch, and so on. The French, being generally the most numerous, had as a rule two houses to themselves. As usual there was no contact between one nationality and the next – they were kept strictly apart. Often there were as many as a hundred men and women under instruction in the various houses.

This was the most vital stage of the entire course. It was no longer physical, but psychological, though no let up was possible in one's physical fitness: that had to be fully maintained. But here, in the main, the mind had to be reconditioned for the work that each secret agent had to undertake in enemy-occupied territory.

The staff of instructors numbered about twenty. Some were business men, others were travelling salesmen, schoolmasters, lawyers and journalists. One was an actor. Each of them was fluent in one at least of the European languages, in addition of course to French and German; and always among the instructors there were those who had a knowledge of the particular country to which some of the agents were to be sent – such as Greece and Norway and Yugoslavia.

The classes for the most part were small, consisting of only three or four pupils; occasionally there was just one pupil, for some of the instruction had to be given individually. Since hardly anything of this kind had ever been attempted before in any previous war, the bulk of the course had to be most carefully evolved, and it was constantly being expanded or modified to suit the ever-changing requirements of the situation as revealed by the experience of our agents on the other side.

The overall essential was to provide oneself with a completely new identity, one which would help the secret agent to merge entirely into the life of the district in which he or she was going to live. A cunningly forged identity card would be provided of course, as well as food coupons and clothing coupons. These were indispensable tokens. In addition one had to hold in one's mind the details of the entire life of the new

Violette at the age of nine. This picture was taken by a photographer at Abbeville while she was staying in France with her Aunt Marguerite.

Violette's parents – Mr and Mrs Charles Bushell. He is English, was in the regular army. During the first world war he met Mlle Renée Leroy in the village in France in which he was billeted. They were married at Pont Rémy, near Abbeville in Northern France, in 1918. Violette, their second child, was born in Paris on June 26th, 1921.

The house in Brixton in which Violette lived with her parents. It is No. 18, Burnley Road. Violette's room was on the first floor.

The London County Council School in Stockwell Road, Brixton, to which Violette went at the age of eleven. It was just round the corner from her home. There were about a thousand children, boys as well as girls; about a third of them were juniors. "Physical Violette was very strong," her teachers say. There was no drain pipe she could not climb, no wall she could not scale.

A holiday snapshot taken when Violette was fifteen. She is seen with her elder brother Roy.

Another holiday snapshot with her brother. Every form of acrobatics appealed to her.

Violette loved rock climbing and all other forms of tough sport, including shooting, at which she was a good deal better than her brother.

The water fascinated her too. She was an extremely good swimmer and was also very fond of boating.

Violette with her father Charles Bushell at Aldershot on the day Etienne Szabo proposed, asking Papa, first in French, then in dumb show, for her hand in marriage.

Violette a a teenager – a snap taken in London just before the outbreak of war. She was working at the time at Woolworth's on Oxford Street, just opposite the Academy Cinema.

The wedding picture, taken immediately after Violette's marriage to Etienne Szabo at Aldershot on August 21st, 1940. After a very brief honeymoon he left for Abyssinia to fight with the French Foreign Legion against the Italians.

Etienne and Violette – a honeymoon snap, taken in the garden of their hotel at Aldershot.

A card from Etienne Szabo sent from Durban in South Africa to Violette's aunt. He signs himself 'Stephen' because of the difficulty some of the family had over his Christian name Etienne.

Violette at the time she became a secret agent. She had been in the Land Army, then joined the ATS and served in an anti-aircraft battery just outside Liverpool, and later worked in an aircraft factory at Morden in Surrey.

Wanborough Manor, near Guildford in Surrey, adjoining a little village called Normandy. Here Violette began her training as a secret agent in 1943.

Violette at Bournemouth in a bath chair, convalescing after the injury to her left foot while undergoing her parachute course at Ringway, near Manchester.

Charles Staunton, who was French by birth and had been a journalist in Paris before the war. He became a secret agent and went out with Violette as her leader on both her missions to France.

Part of a letter written by Violette to Robert Mortier, just before leaving on her first mission.

Samedi soir
11 Mars 1944

Cher Bob
Je suis honteuse
de moi même de n'avoir
pas répondu à tes très
longue lettres j'espère que
tu m'excusera.

J'espérais te

31 Si tu veux bien me laisser savoir quelle jour tu retourne je pourrais te dire où tu peu me trouver j'espère que tu es en bonne santé; merci pour les lettres

Bons Baisers

Violette

P.S
Mes frères envoient leur meilleurs souhaits

Robert Mortier, as he was in 1943, at the age of twenty. The picture was taken just before his mission to Rouen, which preceded Violette's solo mission to Rouen and Le Havre.

Carte d'Identité

NOM *Leroy*

Prénom *Corinne Reine*

Profession *Secrétaire Commerciale*

Né le *26 Juin 1921*

à *Bailleul*

Département *Nord*

Nationalité *Française*

Domicile *64 rue Thiers*
Le Havre

SIGNALEMENT

Taille *1m 64*
Cheveux *châtains*
Moustache
Yeux *marrons*
Signes particuliers *néant*

Dos *rect*
Nez }
Dimensions *moy.*
Forme du visage *ovale*
Teint *mat*

Empreinte digitale

Le Titulaire,

Les Témoins,

5 MAI 1943 .19

Violette's faked identity card, used by her during her first mission to France, when she was landed in the south-west of Paris in April 1944. With this card she went into Rouen and to Le Havre, in the German forbidden zone which was part of the Atlantic Wall.

The poster Violette found on the wall in a street in Rouen. The wanted men were her friends and colleagues, *(left)* Staunton, who was waiting for her in Paris, and *(right)* Bob Mortier, who was to go with her on her second mission later that year.

The secret aerodrome at Tempsford, near Sandy in Bedfordshire, from where Violette set out on both her missions.

MOLYNEUX
SOCIETE A RESPONSABILITE LIMITEE &C°
AU CAPITAL DE 950.000.000
PARIS
5.RUE ROYALE
TÉLÉGRAMMES MOLYROYALE-PARIS
TÉLÉPHONE ANJOU 02 21 · 7 Lignes
LONDRES
CANNES · BIARRITZ
MONTE-CARLO
R C SEINE 152 816

Paris le 28 avril 1944

Mademoiselle C. Leroy

Robe 17 en crepe noir	(104909)	9.500.
Robe 37 en écossais	(15879)	9.000.
Golf jersey jaune	(15879)	6.500.
Robe 45 en imprime	(15897)	9.000.
		32.000.
Taxe le transaction majorée 11,11%		3.355
		35.355
Taxe municipale 1% ·	....	320.
Taxe au profit du secours national 5%		1.800.
		37.475

Alice/L

This bill from Molyneux in Paris indicates the purchases made by Violette, in her assumed name of Mlle Leroy, at the end of her mission to Rouen and Le Havre, and just before returning to England.

Hasell's Hall, near Sandy in Bedfordshire. Here Violette dined and stayed for two nights because of the delay in starting on her second mission.

The grocer's shop in Sussac, above which Violette lived during her second mission to France. It is in the Haute Vienne, about twenty miles to the south of Limoges.

Anatasie. His real name was Jacques Dufour. Though only twenty at the time, he was such a formidable foe that the Germans called him "the biggest bandit of all the Maquis in the Limoges area." He and Violette were together in a car when the German troops ambushed them. Violette's heroic stand against the Germans enabled Anastasie to escape.

The scene of the ambush in Salon-la-Tour. The Germans were crouching behind the hedge at the end of the road, just beyond the white road sign. Anastasie's sharp eyes spotted their presence there and he pulled up the car just by the bicycle on the left of the picture.

Anastasie lay flat in a shallow ditch on the left of the road; but Violette crossed to this tree and, standing under it, fired with her Sten gun at the Germans as they emerged from the ambush and came to capture her and Anastasie.

Violette and Anastasie were chased for two miles across these fields and meadows, which dip down to a stream in which Anastasie used to paddle and fish as a child. As the far end can be seen the cornfield in which Violette fell.

The cornfield, which is seen ploughed up in this picture. After zig-zagging through the tall corn, Violette fell, her ankle badly injured. Anastasie began to carry her, but she struggled, broke away and standing under the smaller of the two trees, blazed away with her gun at the Germans, while Anastasie got away.

It was here, where you see the white hen, that Anastasie hid under a pile of logs. Violette was brought here by her German captors. The two armoured cars came up here, too, and she was taken off in one of them. Under the bridge runs the main railway line from Paris to Toulouse.

The farmhouse opposite the railway bridge seen in the upper picture. The farmer and his wife witnessed the chase and the scene with the Germans that followed. Anastasie had been to school with their two daughters. When he emerged from under the logs very late that night, it was in this farmhouse that he was hidden.

The jail in Limoges in which Violette was confined after her capture at Salon-la-Tour. From here she was taken twice a day by two guards to the Gestapo Headquarters for questioning.

The Gestapo Headquarters in Limoges. It was in a street off the square in front of the jail. After the surrender of the Germans in Limoges a few weeks later it became the headquarters of the British, and her friends Staunton and Mortier moved in here.

The entrance to Fresnes Prison, just outside Paris, where Violette was taken from Limoges and kept a prisoner until her transfer to Ravensbrück.

The sinister entrance of the Gestapo Headquarters in Paris at No. 84, Avenue Foch, where Violette was brough in a Black Maria and tourtered.

Fritz Sühren, the Commandant of the Women's prison camp at Ravensbrück.

Schwartzhuber, the deputy commandant of the prison camp at Ravensbrück. The picture was taken in the military court at Hamburg early in 1947 at the time of his trial. He was found guilty and hanged.

A sketch made by Violette Lecoq, who was a prisoner in Ravensbrück at the same time as Violette Szabo. The picture shows the two-tiered bunks on which the women slept, five and six to a bunk.

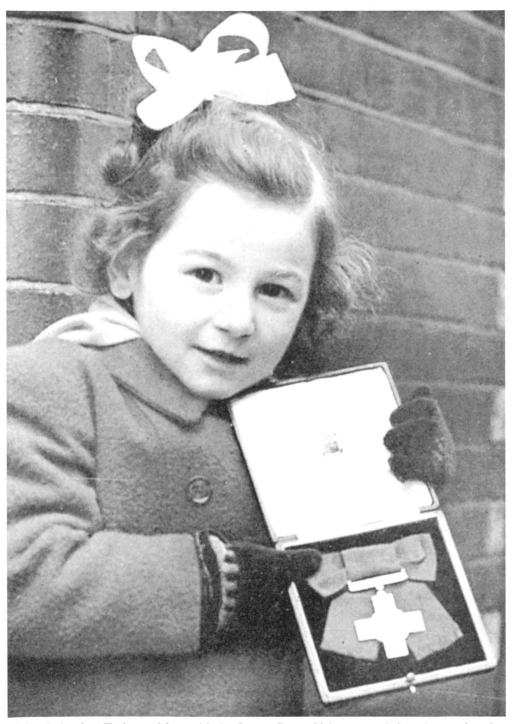

Violette's daughter Tania, aged four, with the George Cross which was awarded posthumously to her mother. It had just been handed to her by King George the Sixth. As she came out of Buckingham Palace with her grandparents, the photographers gathered round and asked her to open the case and hold it out.

Tania, held up by Odette Churchill to look at the tablet unveiled at St Paul's Church, Knightsbridge, by Princess Alice on May 7th, 1948. It bears the name of Violette Szabo, G.C., together with those of other brave women in the same service who died during the last war. Odette says: "While I held Tania in my arms, I could not help feeling that it might so easily have been the other way round – Violette holding up my child, with my name instead of hers on the tablet."

Tania as she is today at the age of fourteen. The picture was taken in Australia, where she lives with her grandparents, Mr and Mrs Charles Bushell.

personality – incidents, for example, of one's childhood and one's work (both fictitious), a familiarity with the fresh setting and with the events of recent years. The Germans had been in occupation for three and a half years. Their military police and the Gestapo, as one was aware, kept a keen, searching eye on all activities that seemed in the least unusual and were only too readily aided by French men and women who were anxious to curry favour. There were restrictions and regulations with which Violette would have to become familiar. There were all sorts of shortages, which did not necessarily correspond with those in England. As a member of the community, as one who was supposed to have lived there continuously, she would have to know something also about the trains and buses, both of which had been greatly reduced, and she would have to avoid showing any surprise with what was really unfamiliar. In this setting she would be not Violette Szabo, but someone with a new name, a new background, and a new job, an undercover girl, quite apart from her actual work as secret agent. She was told that it was not at all like assuming a role on the stage and learning lines that she could trot out as required. One could be a bit too pat, which, of course, one never was in real life. The date of one's birth one knew, but there were little incidents in one's actual life that one had to search the memory to recapture.

This assumed identity was rehearsed over and over again. In the small hours of the morning two men, taking on the role of the Gestapo, would enter the house in which Violette lived, shake her out of a deep sleep and question her closely. Slips were inevitably made the first time, and by many even at the second rapier-edged grilling. Violette fared no better than the rest. Imagine yourself trying drowsily, to put over a pack of lies to two keen-witted men with the power of life and death over you. It is not easy. Hence the need for the recurrent rehearsals. They served to make the mind alert, the tongue less hesitant, the manner less awkward and much more natural.

Another important lesson was on how not to attract attention to yourself. One began with the assumption that almost any-body might be hand in glove with the Germans. It might be a

French girl, an old woman, a farm hand, an errand boy – the least likely passer-by or shopper might have a wary eye open to detect and to tell. It might be someone in a window across the road. So you had to be extremely circumspect and yet not show by a move or a glance that you were trying to make sure you weren't being watched. You had to walk quite unconcernedly and still keep your senses alert. If you felt you were being followed you had to know the best method of eluding the follower. That is what you were taught in this course and you had to put it into operation in a series of testing rehearsals. These were generally carried out at Bournemouth or some other near-by town. You were taken there by car and left at a street corner. Someone you didn't know was tipped off to follow you. You had, by applying the instructions received in the course of the training, to make your way back to your own house without being caught up by the man or woman who was following. This too was tried out again and again. In films the person under suspicion is generally seen standing flat against a dark wall, with both arms outspread and, presently, the pursuer goes by without noticing. That, by its very unusualness, would in fact attract attention if done in enemy-occupied territory.

These exercises began to square up with some of her ideas about spying. What was even more exciting was a reversal of the procedure when she had to be the active instead of passive person. She had to do the looking-out, the watching and the detecting. She had to seek for slips and false moves so as to determine which of the men and women around her were to be suspected. As a prelude to this she was taught, with photographs, charts and diagrams, the entire German military and espionage set up – the uniforms of the Nazi army, the air force and the police, all the German divisional signs, even the lorry registrations, and whatever had been discovered of the methods of the Gestapo, the Abwehr, who were concerned with intelligence and counter intelligence, and other organisations which wore no uniform, their mode of communication by codes and ciphers, their aim, and the mentality of the German intelligence men and women. These had to be known in order to be circumvented.

She had in these exercises to make contact for her part with people who were prepared to help secretly, and would have to be identified with the greatest possible care so that the enemy, having learned some of her plans, should not, by putting in a substitute, get her into their trap. The process of identification had to appear to be perfectly natural. The greeting exchanged might be overheard, so it had to be commonplace, yet it had to have inserted into it, in a way that would not make the eavesdropper prick up his ears, two or three significant words that had been agreed upon, and the response to the greeting would, in the same way, have to be identifiable by special words. Such a remark as "I hope your aunt is better" might evoke the very natural answer, "Yes, much better, thanks for inquiring" – but it would not perhaps be what you were seeking for purposes of identification. The phrase "Lovely day, isn't it?" would have to be discarded, since it might be raining at the time of meeting. It was by no means easy in view of all the pitfalls lying between a natural casualness and security. One had to smile, however serious one's purpose, and perhaps even laugh in order to be disarming, since people engaged in genial converse arouse less suspicion.

The passing on of messages, they were told, could be done in a variety of ways. By word of mouth was the most usual, but to indicate the exact location of a factory or the section of railway lines to be blown up, one had to supply a diagram or an address, and for this one had to resort to the use of paper. A trusted tobacconist or grocer or bookseller handed it on as a receipt or a bill – or it was scribbled on to the margin of a newspaper and thrown down casually on the café table at the moment you were leaving and the new customer, who was to be its recipient, was about to sit down.

Since theoretical instructions were never regarded as enough all this was put into operation in this country. Violette was sent to Southampton, where she had to go along the streets and try to spot those who seemed at all doubtful, to make contacts, to pass on messages – all without detection; and, since an extensive course in sabotage was included in the lessons, she was sent further afield to blow up a bridge or a railway line and try to discover military secrets at air or naval bases in England. The police were not tipped off in advance, and indeed only one high-ranking police officer in each area where these schemes were worked out knew what was going on. The agent would only reveal himself to this officer when all hope of escape was lost. Telephone contact with the police liaison officer at SOE then established his or her bona fides and release followed at once.

Violette was an extremely apt learner. She was at Beaulieu from the end of November 1943 until the first week in February 1944; then she went home to Brixton for a brief rest. She looked extremely fit and was in high spirits. A fortnight later she left **for** Ringway to complete her course in parachute jumping.

Chapter 11

Ready to Go

It was at Ringway that she met Staunton. He was known as Captain Charles Staunton and was regarded as an Englishman. In fact he was a Parisian by parentage and by upbringing. His real name was Philippe Liewer. He was a journalist by profession and worked for the Havas news agency in Paris before the war. Sent to Munich in the autumn of 1938 to cover the famous meeting between Hitler and Chamberlain, which Daladier and Mussolini also attended, he was turned back at the airport by the Nazis and sent home in the next plane. On the outbreak of war he was appointed liaison officer to the British Expeditionary Force and, evacuated from Dunkirk in one of the little ships, was brought to England, but returned to France to see his wife. He had told her "I'll come back whatever happens to France." And he did, though, with the swift and dramatic developments, endless difficulties inevitably presented themselves and had somehow to be overcome. His wife, a journalist and a novelist who wrote under the name of Marie Louise Villiers, had left Paris, he discovered, and was at Nice. So to Nice he went to say his farewell. He found there, although the Germans were not yet in occupation of that part of France, a deep feeling of resentment against Pétain and Laval for allowing the Germans to take over half of their beloved country and hold in thrall the lives and happiness of the people. Staunton organised at Nice one of the first Resistance groups in all France. When Pétain's police discovered this, they arrested Staunton and threw him into a Vichy detention camp. It did not take him long to work out a plan of escape. Together with twelve other prisoners he was about to break out when two warders came up, not to detain them, but to beg to be allowed to accompany them. Not together, but split up into small groups of two or three, they crossed the Pyrenees into Spain, and from Portugal they managed to get to England. That was in the autumn of 1942. He contacted the French section of SOE and soon became one of Buckmaster's secret agents. He was given a commission in the British Army (general list), assumed the name of Charles Staunton and went into training for the work that lay ahead. But he missed Ringway. He did not like parachute jumping, explained his phobia to Buckmaster and was allowed to skip it.

He was in his early thirties, good-looking, of medium height, had an extremely alert mind and a fine organising ability. In March 1943, his training over, he was sent to Rouen which, because of its position so near the mouth of the Seine, between the two most suitable landing beaches for the Allied armies, was a most vital area. It was the centre of road, rail and canal communications. It was a port for sea-going vessels and a refitting depot for German U-boats, more admirably suitable for this purpose than Le Havre because it was further away from the Channel. Obviously much could be done in this key centre by careful organisation.

Staunton was landed by plane in a field near Blois, many miles to the south-west of Paris. He knew Claude Malraux, a brother of Andre Malraux, the famous French writer, and felt that by contacting him, he might be able to learn of some reliable people with whom he could get a Resistance group started in Rouen. Malraux said he had a brother there named Serge and suggested that Staunton should go and see him. In the succeeding months, Staunton, with the help of Serge Malraux, was able to build up a powerful underground organisation in Rouen. Normally Resistance groups numbered no more than five or six members, of whom none knew more than one or two, so that if caught and tortured they would be unable to give more than one or two away. But in this vital centre, taking in Le Havre and all the intervening country, Staunton was able to build up a vast network of little circuits, numbering in all ninety-eight underground Resistance workers. It took time of course. A wireless operator, Peter Newman, was flown out to him from England in April with his own small transmitting set. A special wave-length was allotted for his signals, a code was supplied, and the hours at which he was to send messages were allocated. Through Newman requests were sent for arms, explosives, and for an instructor to train the Resistance workers. The supplies arrived and with them, also dropped by parachute, came Robert Mortier, who was to be very closely associated with Violette's work later on.

Mortier was not his own name any more than Staunton's was. He was a Frenchman, born in Paris in 1923, the son of French parents, both of whom were teachers and had spent some years lecturing at the University of Columbia in New York. There his elder brother Jacques was born. Robert, called Bob even at home after his parents' long stay in America, was only seventeen when the Germans came to Paris. He was still at school; his parents were in the South of France. Studies, as may well be imagined, were greatly disturbed and, just before the Germans came, the schools closed down. Bob left Paris on a bicycle. The roads were blocked with traffic, which crawled at the pace of the slowest vehicles. There were children in prams, old men and women in donkey carts, others, bowed under their loads, moved along on foot, weeping as they went. At intervals German planes zoomed overhead, dropped their bombs and, as the people scattered into the fields or lay down in ditches, the planes returned and machine-gunned them. By the time Bob reached the south, France had fallen and he was as disgusted with the Pétain-Laval state of affairs as Staunton. His one resolve now was to get out and carry on the fight. He made his way to Marseilles, got a boat to North Africa, joined the French Air Force there, and was sent to Tunisia, where, to his disgust, the Pétainist influence was strong. He was determined to get out of this place too. When the Germans came to Bizerta, he borrowed his colonel's bicycle and cut westward across the frontier to join the Allies, who had landed on the day before at Algiers. He offered his services to a British officer he met in the street and, after the necessary security check-up, he was flown to Gibraltar and shipped from there to England. It was felt that he would be most useful as a secret agent and, after being given a commission in the British Army, he began his training, with an extended course in arms and explosives. It was in this capacity that he was sent to assist Staunton at Rouen. They worked well together.

In December Staunton, as he was leaving to return to England, said to Bob: "The man who has been forging all our papers for us was telling me that he has never seen a parachute landing. He has begged to be allowed to come along. I promised to take him, but as I won't be here for the next one, will you take him along with you? Let him see it all happen – the people sent over and the arms and explosives that are dropped." Then he added with a wink, "It'll be good for his morale."

Bob organised it with his usual care and precision. At a garage in Rouen, which the Resistance used as their headquarters, Bob arranged for a lorry on which to bring back all the equipment and stores that were dropped. He asked the lorry-driver to bring the truck to the garage not later than ten o'clock that night because of the curfew, which was at eleven. The man was late. Bob waited and as the minutes ticked by he got uneasy. At a quarter to eleven he decided he could wait no longer. There was just enough time to get out of Rouen without being stopped by the curfew patrols. Without the truck he could not of course bring back the stores. But the arrangements at the secret landing-ground had to be seen to. So he grabbed a motor-cycle that was parked in the garage and, motioning to the forger to jump on behind him, he sped out of town to the landing-ground near Elbeuf. There he would position the men with torch-lights, check over the stores and hide them until they could be collected the following night.

The motor-cycle, with the forger on the pillion, got safely out of Rouen just as the clocks were striking eleven. Bob was travelling along a deserted country road and had not got far when he heard a car coming up behind him. It was approaching at great speed and soon overtook him, then pulled up sharp and motioned to Bob to stop. Inside the car were the German police. Three men promptly leapt out.

The forger jumped off the back of the cycle the moment he saw the car stop. He scampered off the road and fled across the fields. The Germans fired after him, but the man managed to get away. They questioned Bob about him. Feigning ignorance, Bob said he had no idea who the man was; it was just someone who thumbed a ride.

"You have never seen this man before?"

"Never," Bob assured them.

They thereupon asked him what he was doing out of doors after curfew. He was ordered to remount his cycle and one of the German police got on the pillion behind him. With his revolver at the back of Bob's neck, the German directed him to turn round and drive back to Oissel, a little town four miles outside Rouen. The police car followed, its headlights turned on to keep the cycle in view. Obviously there could be no funny business.

Arrived at Oissel, Bob was surprised to see lights outside two of the buildings in the centre of the town. One he recognised as the town hall, the other, next door to it, was the police station. The German car now overtook the motor-cycle and made for the police station. Bob, feeling this was his chance, pulled up suddenly, swung the cycle round and as his passenger, who was thrown off, was trying to steady himself, Bob flung the cycle violently against him and ran.

Hearing the scuffle the Germans, who were just alighting from the car, blazed after him with their revolvers. Bob was shot through the lung, but dived into a dark side street and was surprised that the Germans did not come after him. Presumably they had emptied their magazines. But a moment later, with their revolvers recharged, the Germans came briskly down the side street. Bob by this time had dashed across a field and was lying in a ditch full of foul water alongside the railway lines.

With their torches, and later with two police dogs, they searched for him through most of the night, but by lying in the water he managed to escape detection. He lay there for some time after the German police had given up the hunt, his limbs frozen, a stinging, agonising pain in his lung; then, crawling and staggering, every step making his suffering unendurable, he succeeded somehow in covering the few miles to Rouen. Threading his way through the streets, with dawn just about to break and reveal his agony to the early passers-by, he reached at last the block of flats in which he lived. Even that was not the end of his torture, for he had to climb up five flights of stairs.

When he let himself in, the friends with whom he lived, roused from their sleep, were appalled at his condition. A doctor, who was also in the Resistance, was fetched at once.

After a very careful examination, the doctor shook his head and said he did not think Bob could live. It was indeed a miracle that he was alive now. They were all greatly overcome at hearing this. The doctor himself, who was very attached to Bob, spared two tablets of his precious sulphanilamide, knowing that they could not now be of any avail. It was an emotional offering to a dying man.

The friends were confronted now with a fresh and extremely grave problem. If Bob were to die there would have to be a funeral. The Germans would be curious. They would examine the body in case it was a ruse of some sort, and, discovering the wound, would pounce on the friends with whom Bob had been staying as a cousin. They would be grilled and tortured, perhaps even shot as members of the Resistance in this vital sector of Germany's coastal defences. They pleaded with the doctor, who was alarmed for himself too, but he said there was no hope at all.

Arrangements for the funeral were made with the utmost secrecy. They got two potato sacks, slit them open and stitched them together into one large enough to take the body, for Bob was exceedingly tall. They also got stones with which to weight the sack further and arranged with a friendly lorry-driver to call for the body just before dawn, take it well out of Rouen and drop it into the Seine, since it could not be thrown off a bridge in the town without attracting a great deal of attention.

The days dragged by, however, without Bob dying. The doctor came again and again, treated him, but there seemed to be no improvement. The lorry-driver got impatient, not knowing when he would be required. Then unexpectedly Bob began to improve. The doctor exclaimed with astonishment and relief. The 'cousins' exclaimed too and threw up their hands with delight. It was clear now that Bob would live. The doctor said it was the bitterly cold water in which Bob lay for so many hours that cauterised the wound and saved his life. Ten days later he was able to get up and join his friends at a New Year's Eve party.

Shortly afterwards Staunton returned to Rouen. He was not expected back so early. He explained that, because of the weather, he had not got a plane to England on the appointed date in December, and would have to wait now for the January moon, for it was only by the light of the moon, within the span of a few days on either side of the full moon, that pilots on these secret trips were able to pick out the landmarks to the isolated fields used for landing.

Staunton was greatly concerned about Bob's condition and insisted on his coming back to England to convalesce. "You must get out, Bob. You've had a pretty bad time and, in any case, you cannot operate here. You are known to them. They would pick you up."

Bob agreed to accompany him. They set out together to get the plane in January, but once again no plane came. This time Staunton refused to let Bob return to Rouen. "You stay in Paris till the February moon. I'll join you there a little before that."

They got their plane on the night of February 6th, 1944, and were flown back to England. One of the first things Staunton did was to go to Ringway. "I must try the jump!" he said. "I can't bear these long train journeys half across France. The parachute brings you much nearer to your objective." And that was how he came to meet Violette.

When she and Staunton returned to London, Bob, who was resting for a while before going on an extended arms course at a school in Hertfordshire, joined them on their first evening in town. He found Violette delightfully refreshing. She was gay and amusing and, now that her ankle was all right, she was able to dance again. He thought she danced divinely. Evening after evening the three sat in her flat and were joined by others who dropped in. Among them were many they had met at one or other of their schools of training. Others were chance acquaintances in army or air force uniforms. They sat talking, drinking, smoking, singing the choruses of various songs, swapping yarns, laughing, while they waited for the next assignment, and varied it by going round to restaurants, cinemas and night clubs. Suddenly one of them would be missing. He had gone without a word, and as suddenly somebody else would loom across their horizon. Fresh friends were made almost every day. You met them at the Studio Club or on the crowded dance floor of the Astoria or one of the night clubs and it was possible that you would never see them again.

She met Harry Peulevé at a much earlier stage, long before her meeting with Staunton and Bob. He was dancing with the widow of a Battle of Britain pilot, an Italian girl whom Violette knew slightly. Harry, despite his name, was English. He was an officer in the British Army, tall, broad-shouldered and very good-looking. Violette was not in uniform at the time. Harry wondered what she was doing in the way of war work, but he asked no questions. Some nights later he ran into her in the underground station at Piccadilly Circus and saw that she had on the uniform of the FANYs. He pointed to it and she explained that she was working in a canteen. She asked if he was on leave. "Yes," he said. "My regiment is to go overseas shortly. Let's have fun while the leave lasts."

They saw a great deal of each other, at times in the company of others, but often alone. They went to the theatre or to a film, dined and talked till three in the morning. Some of her friends wondered if a romance was developing, for her eyes would light up when they danced together and in his there seemed to be more than just a passing interest. Yet neither told the other the truth about their work. This they were to discover some months later when they met under very different circumstances.

Chapter 12

Her First Mission

Staunton, having brought Bob back, was eager to return to Rouen to expand the circuit, check over the details and assign the work that had to be done when the call for action came on D-Day, for that was when they would have to strike at the Germans from behind. It was obvious, of course, that Bob could not go with him. As the German police had caught him once and he had been seen and questioned by four of them his return would involve him, and others too perhaps, in the gravest danger. So it was decided that it would be better for him to operate elsewhere as soon as he was fit again and had completed his present advanced course of training.

Buckmaster felt that Staunton should not go back to Rouen either. Peter Newman, the radio operator, was nominally in charge of the British end there, under Serge Malraux, who controlled the entire circuit all the way up to Le Havre. Help would be sent to Newman during the March moon, but Staunton, Buckmaster insisted, should go elsewhere.

Staunton, however, did not share his view. He wanted to see to the Rouen arrangements himself, as he had started this circuit and knew all the people involved. Buckmaster eventually agreed that, provided Staunton did not enter the area himself, but operated from outside through a reliable, tough and fearless assistant, he could undertake the check in this dangerous area, the whole of which was most rigorously guarded by the enemy. The section formed a vital part of the Nazi Atlantic Wall. It was a forbidden zone, totally barred to all except the actual residents.

97

Violette, Staunton felt, would be his best emissary for this purpose. He mentioned her name to Buckmaster who stared fixedly at him for a while. "Do you feel you could trust her with your life?" he asked at last. "For that's what it amounts to."

"Yes," said Staunton, "I can trust her absolutely."

Buckmaster eventually agreed.

Violette herself leapt at the idea. In order that they should get to know each other better before setting out, Staunton suggested that he might come and stay with her at her parents' house in Brixton for a few days, and, with Mr and Mrs Bushell's consent, he moved in, occupying one of the boys' rooms downstairs.

Mr and Mrs Bushell realised at once, of course, that their daughter was to be sent abroad on what would be not only a dangerous mission, but might even prove to be fatal. They could not discuss or even hint at what was afoot and they tried hard not to show their grave anxiety. By their silence Violette could tell how heavily it was weighing on their minds. She said: "Don't worry, Mama. I'll be back – I promise you I'll come back. And I've been equipped with a wonderful new career. I shall do well at it when the war is over."

Smiling through the tears she was pressing back, Mrs Bushell asked, "And what is that?" – "A cat burglar," said Violette with eyes twinkling. "I can scale walls. I can crack through roofs and blow open safes. There is nothing in that line I can't do." And for the moment the anxiety dissolved in laughter.

Violette went along again and again to Mill Hill to see Tania. The March moon period drew near and the moment came to say goodbye. She and Staunton got ready. Papa asked if he could go part of the way with them. "As far as Victoria Station," she said and there they parted.

With Staunton she went to the headquarters of the French Section of SOE for final instructions. Their forged papers had been prepared and were handed to them. On her new identity card, most skilfully devised on the exact pattern in use in occupied France, she was Corinne Reine Leroy, the surname being her mother's before marriage; her profession, it stated, was *Secrétaire Commerciale.* The date of her birth was entered correctly – 26 Juin 1921, but the place of birth was altered to Bailleul, Départment Nord. Her nationality was put down as French and her domicile – 64 rue Thiers, Le Havre, so that she might have a right of entry in the forbidden zone. The other entries read: Height 1m.64, hair *châtain* or auburn, eyes *marrons,* face *ovale,* colour pale. The card bore her photograph, her fingerprint and her new signature. Her identity number was 98272. The card was rubber-stamped in the appropriate places with a very fine imitation of the Mairie du Havre stamper, overlapping both her photograph and the fifteen franc stick-on stamp pasted under it. The date put on it was May 15th of the preceding year 1943 and it bore the correct rubber-stamped signature, authorising her to be in the forbidden *Kusten* zone or coastal area. Ration cards both for food and for clothing were also provided, with rubber-stamped dates in a variety of faded inks, put on crookedly (as they generally are) for the months when she was actually in England.

A further provision was a set of papers, made out in a different name, to help her to escape through Spain in case the Germans got on to her trail and the British were unable to come to her rescue. The name she was to use in Spain was Miss Vicky Taylor.

A postal address in Spain was also supplied, and a special code (which had to be memorised) provided such innocent words as *un, deux* and *trois* with special significance. *Trots,* for example, meant 'I have gone to my cachette, or hiding-place, as arranged. Come and get me out.' The name she was to use for these messages was 'Louise'. These changes of name were intended to cause confusion and so prevent a possible follow-up by the Germans.

A final check-up was now made on something that Violette and Staunton had been going over together for weeks, with large-scale maps and photographs. From this she had acquired a detailed knowledge of Rouen and of the surrounding countryside in which she was to operate – the names of the main streets, the turnings off them, the shops, the riverside *quais,* the cinemas, the public baths, the buses, especially the country buses of which there were now very few. She had been equipped with a clear and exact mental picture.

With Peter Newman in Rouen, London had been in close radio contact, working out the place and the hour for the parachute drop. Everything, London was informed, had been fully organised. The reception committee would be there, awaiting the arrival of Staunton, whose return they welcomed, and of Violette.

On the day they were to leave, London received a strange and startling message. It came not from Rouen but from a Resistance group in the South of France, the one headed by Serge Malraux's brother, Claude, whom Staunton had contacted on his first trip to France, before going to Serge in Rouen. The message, signed Catherine, claimed to be from a friend of Serge's who had managed to get out of Rouen and make her way down to Claude. She said that the Germans had arrested Serge and Peter Newman, had seized the transmitting set, found the code and had been sending messages in order to get Staunton and whoever else came out with him into their clutches. Catherine's message was brief and urgent. Its phrasing revealed her agitation and her acute distress. "For God's sake don't come," she urged, "or you'll find the Nazis waiting for you on the landing-field." Buckmaster was baffled. All their cautious spade work which had built up a powerful organisation to support the Allies on D-Day in quite the most vital area appeared to have been, if not destroyed, at any rate dented. How much of it still remained? What did these warning messages mean? Who was Catherine? The organisation knew nothing of her. Staunton said he knew her well. She had worked with him all the time he was in Rouen. She was one of the most loyal and reliable members of the vast team he had set up there.

The warning came only just in time. A few hours later and Violette would have been on her way with Staunton, without any means of being contacted and turned back.

Their departure was cancelled of course. They would have to wait now until the next moon in April. The place selected for the drop had to be abandoned. They would have to land at some distance from Rouen, possibly outside Paris. From there Violette would have to make her way up to Rouen in order to find out what had really gone wrong, who had been arrested, how much the Germans actually knew.

There was nothing for Violette and Staunton to do now but to wait for three or four weeks. She went to live in her flat. Friends dropped in. They talked and laughed and dined out. Often she spent the evening with Staunton. Bob joined them when he was able to get up to town. Harry Peulevé had apparently sailed with his regiment for she no longer heard from him or ran into him at their familiar haunts.

Quite unexpectedly she had been given this bonus of time with her daughter Tania and she made the most of it. The child was close on two years old – sweet, pert, talkative and happy. During the long months of training, broken by her period of convalescence, Violette had scarcely had any opportunity of being with her. Now she spent days on end at Mill Hill, leaving her address and telephone number at SOE headquarters in case there was a sudden chance to go.

She was beginning now to know her child. She found that instead of just an animated, smiling, cooing baby, Tania was an individual, with a personality and a will, and she wondered *if* anything happened ... Quickly she checked herself. Of course she would come back. Of that she was quite confident – and they would have months together, years together once this war was over. She insisted on doing everything for the child herself – preparing her meals, carrying her up to bed, sitting beside her and telling her the most fanciful tales, drawn from books she had herself read as a child, and of the places she had been to, and especially of her own childhood in France. She promised to take Tania there one day – and fell silent as she realised that Etienne would not be with them now. "I'll take you to Paris," she said, wrinkling her nose at the child. "I'll take you to the Madeleine." She remembered stopping suddenly on the pavement and pointing up to it and asking her mother what it was – and also that it was there that Etienne had planned to take her ... to give thanks ...

101

These weeks were full of memories and of hopes. Then at last the call came. They were to leave a night or two before the Easter full moon, which fell on April 8th. Violette came up to town some days before in order to go over the plans again with Staunton in case there had been any changes, and to refresh her mind about the places and streets in the Rouen area, and to check carefully, although it had been done very thoroughly before, all the personal articles she was taking with her. The clothes she was to wear had been specially made for her by one of the very few firms engaged in making these clothes for secret agents in the style of the country to which they were being sent. On hers French seamstresses had in worked so that none might detect any difference in cut or in size of stitching. The lining, the buttons, the braid used had all to be right. The jackets worn in France at the time were ten inches longer than in England and there were other minor but far from negligible differences. These clothes were given her some weeks before so that they might be worn and not look new. English laundry marks and name tags had of course to be obliterated. Her face-powder, her toothbrush and toothpaste, her make-up accessories, even her shoe polish (in case she had to clean her shoes after a muddy landing) had all to be such as one could buy in France at that time.

Violette was cheerful and quite calm when she reported at headquarters on the afternoon of the appointed day. Staunton had gone straight on to the aerodrome, but Violette travelled with Vera Atkins by car through the pale waning light to the secret aerodrome in Bedfordshire. As they passed through Mill Hill, Violette leaned slightly towards the window. Seeing that Vera had noticed it, Violette said: "It's where my child is." That was the only hint she gave that Tania was in her thoughts.

"I know she was devoted to her child," says Vera Atkins. "Every moment she could spare she spent at Mill Hill. But she said nothing more to me that evening about Tania. She just sat there calm and composed – the picture, one might almost say, of a poster girl, for she was really very beautiful – the sort of loveliness that churned up the emotions of every man. But she did not seem to be conscious of it at all. She never fussed about the way her hair was done or worried about her make-up. And, despite the havoc she caused among men, she was not in the least bit flirtatious."

Violette was conscious only of the great experience that lay ahead. In a few hours she would be in France. A year ago she did not think this would be possible in war-time. It was another world, remote, completely cut off, and impossible of access ... Not since that night, nearly five years ago, when she bade her aunt goodbye at Calais and scurried on board with her young brother to return to England on the eve of the war, had she seen the beloved countryside of France, and not since she was five had she been in Paris. Etienne had been there since the war – within a few months of their first meeting. Her thoughts roved over all this and the car journey was completed in silence.

They drove to a large and attractive country house near Sandy. It was an eighteenth-century mansion, a few miles from the secret airfield at Tempsford. The house stood well back from the road and was hidden in a wood. By the bar in the large lounge and also at the tables in the dining-room were a number of men, commandos, RAF pilots and special forces officers going out on various dangerous missions. Violette and Vera were the only women there. Staunton came in dressed in slacks and a leather jacket. Over these, before leaving, he was to draw on a flying suit, specially designed with a large number of zipped pockets into which were thrust a revolver, a knife, a small flask, emergency rations, maps, compass, a shovel and other equipment that might be needed if he ran into difficulties. In a belt, against his skin, he carried franc notes to the value of many thousands of pounds. Violette, similarly dressed and equipped, carried French money too in case they got separated on landing. Her francs totalled 100,000, which at the then rate of exchange were worth close on 600 pounds. Secret agents were also offered what was known as an L pill. Its effect was lethal (hence the L) and it was provided in case, in a tight corner, or when facing acute torture, the agent felt he or she could not endure the agony any longer. The pill had to be secreted, generally in a garment, and had always to be at hand. It is a confirmation of Selwyn Jepson's ultimate analysis, following his initial fear that Violette might be suicidal, that she should have refused it. Self-destruction was not even remotely in her mind. Whatever came she was prepared to face it. She declined to take the pill with her.

A final examination followed. Their cigarette-cases were gone through for English cigarettes. Their pockets were searched for matches, forgotten bus tickets or stubs of theatre and cinema tickets. Their identity cards, their rations cards, their clothing coupons were all checked very carefully. Their suitcases, similarly inspected, had already been placed in the plane.

A car with the blinds drawn took them not only on to the airfield but right up to the plane. It was a Lysander, the smallest plane in use at the time, and known familiarly as a 'Lizzie'. It wa revving up in readiness. Hands were shaken, goodbyes said, and the two got in, sitting back to back behind the pilot. Slowly the Lizzie taxied and then took off, heading for France.

Going by Lysander meant that they were not going to be dropped but were to land. So they had no parachutes. The plane was no doubt required to do some Pimpernel work on the other side, to bring back agents, as in the case of Bob, or VIPs whom the Gestapo were after, as well as reports supplementing the brief radio messages. They crossed the Channel at a height of 3,000 feet, then the plane dropped gently down to 400 feet, at which height it was almost impossible for the German anti-aircraft guns to hit it. Its speed was less than 200 miles an hour and, being very small, it was able to land on a field only 30 yards long. Soon the landmarks would be picked up with the aid of the moon, and as it neared the landing-ground, an ultra short-wave wireless set in the plane, called the S phone, would get the directional signal. They would then see the three or four small pinpricks of light flashed by members of the reception committee, carefully spaced out to indicate the size of the field.

The landing-ground selected for tonight lay hidden among farmlands between Chartres and Orleans. Before it could be reached the Lysander was spotted by a German fighter, and after a series of manoeuvres was forced to turn off its course. The Messerschmitt with its great speed kept overshooting them and whizzed by again and again. It was obviously impossible in these circumstances to land, so the pilot turned back. Violette and Staunton, faced with having to wait in England for maybe a further month, wondered, as their plane climbed and recrossed the Channel for home, whether by some cruel fate they were destined not to carry out this operation. But after a while the German fighter gave up the pursuit and their plane, with barely enough petrol left, turned again and retraced its course towards the secret landing-ground.

Suddenly, below them, they saw the dim signalling lights of the electric torches. With the engine switched off, the plane began to descend cautiously, down and down towards the pale moonlit countryside, and in a few minutes was bumping gently along the uneven field.

Silently the men with flashlights ran towards them. As the plane came to a stop, first Violette, then Staunton descended down the steel ladder on the outside and were clasped in a welcoming embrace.

They all talked in whispers. Bicycles had been brought for the two passengers. Their suitcases were taken out of the plane and strapped on to the backs of the cycles: in Violette's case, as she had two suitcases, one of them had to be strapped on to her back. They then set out through the night on a long cycle ride of more than twenty miles. It was not wise to try to go as far as Paris because of the curfew, so they spent what remained of the night in the home of one of the Resistance workers. Supper was insisted on by their host and hostess. A couple of sandwiches and a swig of coffee from a flask in the plane, although it was better coffee than one could get in France at the time, was not considered enough, not by French standards. In any case a meal had already been prepared. In the kitchen, spread out on a table covered with a checked tablecloth, spotlessly washed and ironed, were dishes of delicious *hors-d'oeuvre,* the onion soup was being warmed on the stove, and large steaks had been prepared too, for outside the big towns there was plenty of food in occupied France, especially in a farming area such as Violette was in now. They ate well; the coffee they had brought along from England was enjoyed by all and was followed by a strong cognac.

They slept late the next day and then took a train into Paris.

Chapter 13

On the Normandy Coast

Staunton had an aunt in Paris in the Rue Sts Perès, leading from the Boulevard St Germain to the left bank of the River Seine near the Pont du Carrousel. Just across the river were the Tuileries Gardens and the Louvre. So it was extremely central. Staunton arranged that Violette should live there with her. He himself went elsewhere, for, if the Germans were after him, it would have endangered Violette and his aunt too if he was found there.

Violette had of course been schooled fairly thoroughly in the names of the streets in central Paris. She went exploring on the first day with Staunton's aunt. She glanced at the Eiffel Tower, black against the grey sky. They walked up the Rue Royale, she saw the Madeleine again and her mind was filled at once with thoughts of Etienne and Tania. The streets swarmed with Germans in uniform. Others, unmistakably German, wore ordinary civilian clothes. They were for the most part industrialists hurrying about their affairs or out shopping, for the shops still had much to sell despite the German depredations during the four preceding years. She saw scarcely any motor-cars. Most of the French men and women went about on bicycles. There were bicycle taxis, quaint contraptions that the driver worked with pedals while the passenger sat alongside in a small covered sidecar. There were no buses. The Métro was still running and it was the principal means of transport for long distances.

In a restaurant in the main Boulevard des Capucines, Violette used her forged ration cards for the first time. The meal was expensive and the choice was extremely restricted. Later in the afternoon, as had been arranged, she met Staunton in the Luxembourg Gardens and they talked as they walked along the well-kept paths.

He arranged that she should go to Rouen the next day by the morning train. The distance was about seventy-five miles and the journey now took nearly two hours. Staunton said: "When I went there for the first time to start the Resistance group, I was sure of one contact. I had Serge Malraux. But you have no contacts at all and not even a wireless transmitter to keep you in touch with London. You have just nothing. I've prepared this list of the people who used to be in the group – but we have no idea if they are still there or if they are still with us. You'll have to memorise all this and destroy it. You can't take the list with you. All that you can be sure of is that you are going into great danger. You will hardly be able to move without being watched and followed. It's a pity you have to go alone. But if I came along, it wouldn't help, it would only increase the danger."

"I understand," she said.

"Still want to go?" he asked.

"Yes," she said. "I still want to go – and you may be sure."

"I know," he said, patting her arm. "I know."

He then gave her one last word of advice. "Try not to say very much."

"You don't imagine I'll …"

"It's not that," he said, "but you have quite a marked English accent."

"I have?" She was very surprised.

"Didn't you know? You could get away with it if you said you were from Alsace Lorraine. But the Germans would expect you to know German then. So" – he winked – "don't say much. It's the French who would spot you and you never know which of them you can trust."

Staunton himself was going into other areas to give final D-Day instructions. All would have to play their part when the Allied landings were made. We needed every act of sabotage and organised destruction behind the enemy lines to coincide with these landings. He asked Violette to meet him in the Luxembourg Gardens at the end of the month.

That night she walked alone along the *quais* on the left bank. The river looked lovely in the soft moonlight. She could hear the heavy stamping feet of German sentries. From far away came the sound of flak – heavy flak, firing no doubt at British planes – and she thought she heard even further away the sound of bombs exploding. In her mind she reversed the position and saw herself serving the anti-aircraft guns near Liverpool. Now it was our own planes that were overhead.

In the morning at the Gare St Lazare, as she walked along the platform to her train, she noticed many of the Germans turning to stare at her. For a moment she felt uneasy; was there something wrong about her clothes? But she saw in their widening eyes a stare of appraisal and she walked on unheeding. The train was as crowded as trains were in England in war-time. She had been told that certain compartments were reserved for the Germans. As she passed one of these a German officer bowed and pointing to the door said, in very guttural French: "Why not come in here, Mam'selle? You won't find a seat anywhere else in the train." Smilingly she accepted and found herself in a carriage full of German officers in uniform. They all rose to offer her a seat. She chose one by the window. Cigarette cases were then whipped out. She smiled as she took one and a colonel gave her a light. She enjoyed seeing so many German officers hopping around in respectful attendance. Wouldn't Mama laugh if she knew! And Winnie too! Then she remembered what Staunton had told her. She must not talk. So she kept to just '*Oui*' and '*Non*' and '*Merci*'.

It was a long and fairly silent journey. Only her recurrent smile kept the atmosphere friendly, while through her mind raced bitter, resentful thoughts as she remembered Etienne's death at El Alamein, caused by men like these. But she must not think, she told herself. The hardening look in her eyes would give her away. So she smiled again and turned to stare out of the window at the slightly battered countryside, though much of it looked lovely with the coming of spring.

109

Rouen once belonged to the English – she had been told all this before she came. Hundreds of years ago the English kings also ruled over this part of northern France, English families lived for generations in this charming old town and to this day many of the names are English, though the people who bear them may no longer be conscious of the link. Violette felt that the town, large, modern and industrial though it was, still retained its charm and beauty in the ancient streets and houses at its core. There were *quais* alongside the river, the same river as in Paris, and a most impressive cathedral. She saw the old tower in which Joan of Arc was once imprisoned; from here she was led out daily by the guards to be questioned by her inquisitors, and later, in this market square, she was burnt at the stake.

One of the first things Violette noticed in Rouen were posters in the streets of two 'Wanted' men. On these were pictures of Staunton and Bob Mortier. They were hideous pictures, making the men she knew so well look like criminals. Under each picture was an X, followed in Staunton's case with the words 'Known as Clément' and in Mortier's – 'Known as Mollier, R.' They had got the correct field names but didn't know who the two men really were. Staunton obviously could not have come here without the risk of immediate arrest.

The place bristled with armed Germans. There were machineguns at almost every street corner. Platoons of German troops marched and stamped through the streets. The vigilance was astounding. There was an air of tension, a nervous awareness that D–Day could not now be far away. They knew too that the Allied landings would be made on the beaches on one side of Rouen or the other and they were determined to deny us any help from inside. Nothing of which they were not fully aware could be allowed to go on. Everything had to be harnessed to the war effort, theirs not ours.

What was left of the Resistance here in the *réseau*, as it was called – that was what Violette had come to find out. Were there enough there to give effective help on D–Day? We had to know what we could rely on and what we should have to write off.

It was difficult for her to know where to begin. She had memorised the list Staunton gave her and, wondering what might be her best plan of inquiry, she had decided to see the wives of the men who had worked with the Resistance. Even this was not easy. The women would be suspicious. Some of them, with their husbands in German prisons, might be hostile, might even, though she hardly liked to harbour the thought, give her away to the Germans in return for some concession or favour or possibly the release of their husbands. She would have to be extremely cautious. It was obvious that she could not visit these women in their homes; and it was difficult, without knowing what they looked like, to make any contact with them in the streets.

She made her way first to the garage which Staunton and Mortier had told her had been their headquarters. It was here that the arms and explosives dropped by parachute by English planes were stored behind a false inner wall. One night, just before the Germans arrested Mortier and in the subsequent chase shot him through the lung, a British bomb, falling nearby, blew in the protective wall and left the secret hoard entirely exposed. Arriving there early in the morning, Mortier and other Resistance workers were horrified to see how near the Germans were to discovering their dangerous secret. A new inner wall was built with amazing speed, while garage hands casually guarded the entrance.

But even here Violette was not at all sure which of the old workers remained. Did that man with a wide brow fit in with one of the descriptions Staunton had given her? Or the man with the béret over his left ear? Or the man with blue eyes under shaggy eyebrows? She went in and asked one of the attendants if she could hire a bicycle. She would need one of course. It would be her only means of transport. The man looked her up and down. They did not have one, he said – not one they could spare. She said she'd look in again. And so, making her moves with the utmost circumspection, working in quite casually the password in use only a few weeks before in this area, in the hope that it might evoke a response, she was able, bit by bit, to pick up the threads.

She was appalled by what she eventually discovered. She found that of the ninety-eight members of this Resistance group more than ninety had been traced by the Germans and taken away as prisoners. What had become of them none knew for certain. Some, it was thought, had been sent to Germany. Others were in various prisons in northern France. Roger Mayer, a schoolmaster, who had been in charge of a group at Le Havre, had been taken off to a German prison camp. His wife, however, managed to get out of Le Havre and was now living in Paris. Some of the other wives were still about and it was possible in time for her to contact a few. She contrived even to get into Le Havre. The forged papers with which she had been equipped in London were not considered safe for use in this closely guarded port of the Atlantic Wall; so new papers were obtained for her, the actual forms, and in these her name was entered. She found there a feverish activity. The formidable line of coastal batteries was constantly being strengthened, fresh strong points were being added even now at this late hour. The beaches had live minefields. Even the sea was mined for miles. The Germans were aware that it was a race against time and Rommel came down for periodic inspections from his headquarters at La Roche-Guyon, midway between Paris and Rouen – the same Rommel whose army had been responsible for Etienne's death in Africa.

Violette was stopped and questioned repeatedly and her papers were subjected to constant examination. There were moments when she was sure she was being followed, but she managed each time to elude the pursuer, practising the art she had learned just across the Channel, and she wondered if the seagulls flying overhead had seen her at it there. Twice she was placed under arrest and taken to the police station for prolonged questioning. On the second occasion she was held there for nearly five hours. The Gestapo seemed not at all satisfied with her answers. Was this to be the end of her activities? And what would be her chance of escape from here? She thought of Bob's awful ordeal, thought also of the ninety or more who had been taken away from here and were now in various prisons, many of them in Germany. There appeared to be little hope for her. Again and again the Gestapo questioned her. But Violette, who had a nimble mind and was convincingly inventive, did not panic for a moment. She had shown in childhood her resource in the face of baffling difficulties; and now, by using her wits, by feigning a most charming innocence, she succeeded in making it impossible for them to link her in any way with subversive work. So they let her go.

Night after night Le Havre and Rouen and the adjoining coasts were heavily attacked by Allied bombers. Only a part of this was the selected area for the D-Day landings, the rest was attacked merely to mislead the Germans. All the main roads, railways and bridges for miles around were heavily bombed too in order to disorganise all the approaches and impede the bringing up of reinforcements.

Violette stayed in the area for two weeks. She was on the move all the time, spending a night first with one, then with another sympathiser. How many of these would be prepared to render active aid at the vital hour it was her purpose to ascertain.

Seated in Rouen one evening, in a back room behind locked doors, she heard for the first time one of the BBC's news broadcasts, which were sent out nightly at 7.30 and 9.15. They couched last-minute instructions in the most innocent phrases. Some were as simple as 'the cow jumped over the moon'. Single words, sent in from France, were inserted into the programme on three consecutive nights in order to indicate to the hesitant that the plans being made had the full authority and support of London; and by a similar method it was possible to prove, when, for instance, a substantial sum of money was required, that the agent had been authorised to raise it and that it would be refunded in full after the war. Behind all this seemingly childish nursery talk lay the entire might of the Allied forces preparing for the liberation of Europe. Plans for sabotage were indicated or confirmed in this manner. Parachute drops of arms and men, and the despatch of planes to rescue patriots were also, if necessary, adjusted by such simple pre-arranged phrases; and so 'Aunt Louise is better' might easily mean that the drop would take place that very night.

The Gestapo knew of this, of course. It was their purpose to prevent people listening to these broadcasts, not merely because they did not want them to learn the truth about the progress of the war, but because of the vital instructions hidden in some of the silliest phrases, which of course the Germans could not themselves decipher, but they knew the disastrous effect these had on factories, railways, and generally on the Nazi war plans. That is why they burst into people's homes during these hours of transmission: it enabled them incidentally also to discover who the listeners were and, in an area such as Rouen, everyone in the room was rounded up and placed under arrest.

Her inquiries over, she returned her bicycle to the garage and, making sure that she was not being watched, tore off one of the small posters in the street with the pictures of the two wanted men who were her friends. Imagine yourself doing that even in England. Then she took a train back to Paris to report to Staunton at the time and place arranged.

He met her again in the Luxembourg Gardens, where, as they walked, she told him all she had learned. There were many in Rouen and a few in Le Havre, she said, ready and eager to assist in every possible way. They awaited instructions and Violette was ready to return and assist them.

Staunton reflected in silence for a while. "I'm afraid," he said at last, "there won't be enough time to get it all going again. We would have to start completely from scratch. We shall need a radio operator, an instructor, more arms and explosives – for all that we have assembled so painstakingly there over many months has gone – all of it. It would take weeks – many weeks. And D–Day is not so far away now."

"But surely," she said, "if a start is made ..."

"There isn't the time," he repeated. D–Day was in fact less than six weeks away. "But," he added, "at least we know how things are there. We can't call on Rouen, but, as a result of what you have learned, we shall be able to draw on other nearby organisations and fly in people for special jobs, like points to attack and bridges to blow up, when the landings are made. Thanks, Vi. You've done a fine job of work. No one could have done it better."

"What do we do now?" she asked.

"Well – we'll have to be going back."

"When do you think that will be?"

"As soon as we can get a plane. Possibly in three or four days. I'll get through to London this afternoon and see what can be arranged. Take the next two days off. See something of Paris. Go shopping. I'm sure there are one or two things you'd like to buy. Any money left? Well, don't worry about that. I have some over. You've earned the break. Meet me here again in forty-eight hours."

Violette was very tired. The strain of her two weeks in the heavily guarded coastal zone in Normandy, on the alert all the time without any let up, had begun to tell. She was staying again in the Rue Sts Perès with his aunt and when she left Staunton she went straight to bed. In the evening she and Staunton's aunt sat at a table on the Champs Elysées and ate a sandwich with their coffee.

Out shopping by herself the next day, she went to Molyneux, the famous couturier in the Rue Royale, which, despite the German occupation, was still carrying on. The bill head proclaimed quite bluntly that the firm had a branch open in London. Here she bought, as her bill dated April 28th, 1944, shows, three dresses and one very attractive jersey. The bill, made out to Mademoiselle C. Leroy, states that one of the dresses was of black crêpe de chine – it was draped with a lace neckline and cost 8,500 francs. There was, of course, no official rate of exchange between England and France at the time, but the franc was worth much more than it was later: at the pre-war rate of 176 francs to the pound, the cost of this dress works out at nearly £50. Another of the dresses is set down as *'en écossais'*: it was a red plaid dress. The third was of silk print. The jersey, described as a golf jersey, was yellow in colour. The total bill, with a purchase tax of eleven per cent, a municipal tax, and a 'Taxe au profit du secours national' of five per cent, came in all to over £200.

The dresses were fitted. Slight adjustments were required. "Will Mam'selle come back?" she was asked.

"How long will they take?"

"About three days."

"Can you do it in two?" she said. "I have to go to the South to join my parents."

"In two then, Mam'selle. In the afternoon."

She would have liked to have bought a dress for Tania. Dared she order one here? The risk was great. The 'Mam'selle' had been used repeatedly by the salesgirl and it was stressed even on her bill. There would be questions such as, "Can you bring the child in for a fitting, Mam'selle? ... Next week perhaps?" More questions and Heaven alone knew what else.

Walking on towards the Madeleine, which rose in massive magnificence before her, she could almost hear Etienne speaking to her. Her eyes began to fill with tears, she felt she could not keep them back. Hurrying her pace a little, she climbed up the wide flight of steps, swept past the fluted pillars and, plunging into the church's dark interior, got down on her knees and buried her face in her hands. She stayed there for a while, alone with her thoughts of her husband and her child, praying that Tania was well and did not need her. She felt so desperately cut off. No news could be got through to her if the child was ill. She thought of the mother in Rouen in the house in which she had been staying who had to dash out in the middle of the night for a doctor.

She rose, feeling utterly desolate, and walked slowly out into the sunshine. At the side of the Madeleine, leaning against the church, stood the gay stalls of the flower market, with their gorgeous display of spring blooms. Among the daffodils and the tulips were early roses such as Etienne never failed to buy for her. She went to the stall and bought herself three roses. With them in her hand she crossed the road to the Trois Quartiers to get some little trinkets for her mother, for Vera Atkins and for Tania. But she hardly glanced at the varied display as she swept past the counters. Walking boldly up to an attendant, she asked where she could buy a dress for a child aged two. She was directed to the second floor. The choice was restricted. There were not many children in Paris now, she was told. The miniature dresses in pale blues and pinks fascinated her. In her mind she dressed her child in each of them in turn.

As the attendant's voice brought her back to reality, she asked: "Have you nothing smaller? It's for a girl not quite two."

"No, Mam'selle," the attendant said. "We have not much these days. This – and this one here – *très, très gentil.*" They were all for girls who were older. She selected one at last. It was of gay flowered silk, with tiny pink and blue flowers and green leaves against a white background, and had a smocked bodice; in it she felt the sallowness of Tania would be set off to perfection. But she would have to wait a year or two before she could wear it. When she was four perhaps. Violette saw herself leading the child by the hand as they set off together for perhaps her first party.

"I'll take that," she said. Her heart was lighter now. She felt more cheerful. For her mother she bought some perfume, a compact, a pretty scarf and a pair of black gloves; for Vera Atkins she got a pendant brooch with three small and one large cluster of red and green enamel beads, a pearl at the end of each cluster.

The next day, when she saw Staunton, she learned that they were to be picked up the following night by a Lysander from a field near Blois. That would mean leaving Paris by train in the afternoon. It meant also calling for her dresses at Molyneux a little earlier than arranged.

They were met at Blois station by two men with bicycles. They had to pedal through the darkness for an hour with their suitcases strapped on behind them, and in her case also a large box containing the purchases she had made. The patriots with flashlights said their farewells and guided the plane out.

Chapter 14

Home

The flight home was smooth and without incident. The Lysander landed at Tempsford aerodrome shortly before dawn and a car brought them into London.

Staunton accompanied Violette to her parents' home in Brixton. The neighbourhood had not yet begun to stir. All was still in the house when the bell rang. The Bushells, wondering who could have rung it at that early hour, turned over in bed. Mr Bushell looked at his watch. Mrs Bushell, almost aware who it might be, got out of bed and went to the front door. Her hair was in disarray. She was tying the cord round her dressing-gown as she slid back the bolts. When the door opened she saw only a man standing there. "I've brought your daughter back," he said. Craning forward she saw Violette leaning wearily against the wall. "She was all in," says Mrs Bushell.

"Just put her to bed," said Staunton. He declined the invitation to come in for a cup of coffee.

Violette said: "I could sleep for a week."

"Come up to bed, darling." With her arm around her daughter's waist, Mrs Bushell led Violette into the house. They were confronted by the entire household in the hall. Mr Bushell was there and his sister Florence, who had come up from Hereford to meet her son Norman, home on leave from the Navy; and Norman was there too – all avid to see and to greet Violette.

"All right," she said. "I'll have a coffee with you before I go up to bed."

They sat in the kitchen and in their eager questioning kept her talking for two hours. She said nothing of Rouen or her work, merely that she had been in Paris. She could not resist telling them of the Germans who kept offering her cigarettes and insisted that she should share their compartment in the train. She did it with vivid mimicry, imitating their clumsy French accents, their heel-clicking and bowing and their heavy politeness. The suitcases were then brought in and unpacked. The Molyneux dresses were greatly admired. Mama fingered the material, examined the cut and the finish. They all cooed over the dress she had brought back for Tania. Mama was especially thrilled with the gifts Violette had got her. She tried on the Paris gloves, sniffed the perfume approvingly, gazed with admiration at the compact. To Aunt Florence Violette gave one of her own bottles of perfume.

By now the feeling of acute fatigue seemed to have left her. She refused to go to bed. All she wanted was a bath. After it, she was glad to be able to put her uniform on again and made her first call at the headquarters of the French Section of SOE. There she ran into a secret agent who was getting ready to leave that night for France. "May Day," he grumbled. "Everybody else has today off – only you and I have to work."

"Mine's finished," she said. "I just got back."

Staunton came out of an inner room. He had just handed in his report. "I've arranged for Bob to dine with us at the Studio Club tonight. I hope you can join us there?"

She said she would be delighted to. "I may be a little late. I'm now off to see Tania." A glow of happiness lit up her face.

All that afternoon she spent with her child. It was a joyous reunion. All the pent-up emotion poured out of her. She told the child of the dress, of the Eiffel Tower, of the Madeleine, and of the wonderful places she was going to take her to when the war was over.

In the evening Bob and Staunton had to wait the best part of an hour for her. "I'll never forget her entry," says Bob. "Everyone turned to stare at her. She looked radiant and very lovely. She had on a red dress she had bought in Paris" – it was the *robe en écossais*. "She was wearing a pair of new earrings she had also got in Paris – they were bunches of red flowers dangling from a gilt chain – and, though she was very sparing as a rule with perfume, that night she seemed to have splashed it on because it was something one could no longer get very easily in England. All the women in the room raised their nostrils to breathe it in and shut their eyes in ecstasy at the heavenly scent. She really looked wonderful."

As she took her seat Violette, her eyes dancing, said: "Wouldn't they be startled if they knew where I have been and where I got it all?"

In Paris now, as they all three knew, though the shops were filled with novelties, one's freedom was greatly restricted. Food and wine and even cigarettes were rationed, one could not dance (the Germans had banned dancing), nor could one move about the town freely at night because of the curfew. After midnight, if you happened to be in a night club, you had to remain there until five in the morning when the curfew ended.

She told Bob of her visit to Rouen and showed him the poster she had torn off the wall with his picture on it.

Bob smiled and shrugged his shoulders. "Well, I'm ready now to be sent off somewhere," he said.

"Don't be surprised," she said, "if I'm back there before you." In point of fact they were all three to make the next trip together in five weeks, but they did not know that yet.

She danced with Staunton and later, while on the floor with Bob, he tipped his head towards the band to draw her attention to what they were playing. It was *The Last Time I Saw Paris.* She looked up at him and smiled.

They went on afterwards to a night club where they stayed till the small hours. Neither Violette nor Staunton seemed to be tired. But they slept through the bulk of the next day.

Her cousin Norman, whom she had not seen for two years, insisted that it would do her a world of good if she came back to Hereford for a few days with him and his mother. She agreed readily and they left a day or two later. There was a fair at Hereford. They went on the roundabouts, to the shooting gallery, where again she won all the prizes, rode in the bumper cars and discovered afterwards that in the course of these boisterous diversions she had lost one of the red flower-earrings she had brought back from Paris. They searched but it could not be found. Her Aunt Florence still treasures the remaining earring, which she insisted on keeping. "Violette used to cook some of our meals," she says. "I remember one night when she was frying eggs. The house was full of a burning smell. She had forgotten to use any fat."

After a week she and Norman, who had to rejoin his ship, came back to town by train. "There were two soldiers in our carriage and Violette and I played pontoon with them for the whole of the journey. She was not normally lucky at cards, but on this occasion she won all the time and was a considerable sum to the good when we arrived at Paddington. She refused to keep it, however, and divided it equally between the two soldiers.

"I spent two or three days in London before going back to sea. Violette knew London well of course, and we had a couple of quite hectic days and nights, finishing up always in a night club, where we danced. She was wonderful company. One evening she stopped our taxi, jumped out and spoke to two men in a car. She did not say who they were, but I guess they were connected with her work, of which she never talked at all." They were in fact Staunton and Bob.

She was fond of staying up late at night, of having lively company around her, of listening to music, and dancing. She did not drink much or smoke heavily. But the need for a release of tension was prevalent in war-time, especially among those serving in the forces. Her mother says: "Violette did not like drink and she smoked very little. One night she took her brother John, who was home on leave from REME, and a young Norwegian named Eric, who was a secret agent, to a night club in Soho. Both boys were over six foot tall, and you can just imagine Violette having to bring them home in the small hours of the morning with one boy on each side of her, holding on for support to this tiny girl. All Violette said afterwards was: 'Somebody had to stay sober or we'd never have got back.'"

As a rule she lived in her flat now, but from time to time spent a night or two at Mill Hill with her daughter. There was a lull in enemy bombing and the buzz bombs had not yet begun to come over. So occasionally she brought the child up to London for the day, took her shopping, and twice took her to SOE headquarters to show her off with pride to Bob and Staunton and the others.

She was told that plans were in progress for the next mission. "You don't have to go," said Buckmaster. "You've done your share – and a fine job it was too. You showed pluck and coolness and great resource."

"Don't you want me to go?" she asked.

"Well, yes. That's up to you. But I feel you ought to know that this time it's going to be much more dangerous."

She smiled. "If I can be of any help, I shall be glad to go again."

Staunton said to her a day or two later, "There's a thought that Bob and I and you might go together. It's going to be very dangerous. Although you've said yes, you can still change your mind, you know."

"Are you trying to drop me?" she asked.

"No. It isn't that."

"What is it then?"

"Just suppose you didn't come back."

"Tell me just this," she said. "Do you think I am capable of …"

"There is no question of that," he interrupted. "You are the one person I feel I can rely on absolutely to do the job."

"Then it's settled," she said. "There's no need for either of us to say any more. I'll come."

He smiled at her. "Good," he said.

"When do we go?"

"At the next moon."

The next moon, the June moon, for which D-Day had been planned too, was less than two weeks off. Many of the people she knew seemed to be away. She ran into very few of them now. The pretty Italian girl she had once seen dancing with Harry Peulevé told her that he was still out of town. "He has gone abroad with his regiment," she said. Where to she did not know.

Violette began to prepare for her own departure. She had a photograph taken of herself. It was not in uniform, but in the pretty black dress draped with a lace neckline which she had bought at Molyneux in Paris. Giving it to her mother, she said: "I like this picture. It's the best one ever taken of me. I'll get some extra copies to give to my brothers, my cousins and a few friends."

Mrs Bushell stared at her for some moments, wondering if there was some sort of presentiment in her mind. Violette merely smiled and wrinkled her nose at her.

A few days later she told her mother that she had made her will. There wasn't much in the bank, just the hundred pounds or so that Etienne had left her, to which had been added her own small salary for the weeks she was away. It would of course continue to be paid in regularly while she was on her next mission. She wanted all the money to be kept for Tania. She also handed her mother the gold bracelet which was Etienne's wedding present to her, an attractive vanity-case she had received in advance for her birthday in June, and her wedding ring. Her engagement ring of emeralds and diamonds she retained. "I'd better keep this," she said. "If I am on the run I should be able to raise some money on it."

She asked her father to dispose of her flat and its contents.

There was some money still to be paid on the refrigerator and the furniture, but Mr Bushell managed to clear it all up and to have £70 over to pay into Violette's bank.

All this made Mr and Mrs Bushell more and more uneasy. It was as though Violette felt uncertain of the future.

She then looked up her friends as though in farewell. She dropped in on Winnie Wilson, who had married two years or so before and was now Mrs Sharpe. "I was doing my washing when Vi dropped in. She was wearing a black cape and a black skirt. With her high cheek-bones she looked very striking. She came to invite my husband and myself to the pictures and stayed only a few seconds, as she was obviously very pressed for time. She insisted that we should be her guests at the cinema. Looking back on it, I realise it was her way of saying goodbye."

Again she went up to Mill Hill for a night or two. Mrs Bushell, who was constantly visiting Tania, promised to keep in the closest touch with the child. On June 4th, just before going to headquarters in readiness for her second mission, Violette went to Mill Hill again and found her mother already there. Mrs Bushell could tell from the warmth of her manner that this was the moment of parting. Violette said: "You are not to worry, Mama. I shall be all right – and if anything should happen, well, Tania will get a good pension. There's a bit in the bank, as you know, and I've made you my executrix. So Tania should really be all right.

"Now there's just one thing more I want to say to you. Things may become difficult out there. I may be on the run and the Germans may be on my track. It may be impossible for me to get back – may even be difficult for me to write. But don't worry, darling, if you don't hear. I'll try – I promise I'll try somehow to get a message through. There may be a way. One can never tell.

"There's just one thing I *don't* want you to do – for Heaven's sake never try to find out where I am. Don't make any inquiries. If you do anything at all, one never knows what it might lead to. It will only add to my danger. You can't help, you know. If you think for a moment you'll realise that you can't really help at all. So don't make a move of any kind. Will you promise, Mummy darling? Just wait until the end of the war – you may have to wait that long. I'll do my damnedest to get back if I'm caught. I'll escape somehow – and quite suddenly you'll find I'm back with you in England."

Her mother's eyes were filled with tears. She did not know what to say. Violette fell silent for a while, then she added, as though thinking aloud: "If they torture me – I wonder if I'll be able to stand it. People do. I hope I will. I think I will."

Mrs Bushell pressed her face against her daughter's. Tania came out to join them.

"You promise?" Violette asked.

Mrs Bushell nodded very slowly.

Then, kissing them both very fervently, Violette moved quickly to the door; but turning there she came back, seized Tania and clasped her close, and kissed her again and again. She broke away at last, hurried up to town and reported at headquarters. There Vera Atkins was waiting with a car to take her to Hasell's Hall, the lovely old Georgian house at Sandy in Bedfordshire, which stood back among the woods and was used as a club house and dormitory by the secret agents and others setting out on special missions.

Chapter 15

Her Second Mission

That, though they did not know it, was the night selected for
the dispatch of the mighty armada taking the invading Allied
armies to the coast of Normandy. They were to land to the west
of Rouen. But the weather all that day had been appalling,
typical of December rather than June. At 9.15 that night, at a
conference at Eisenhower's headquarters in England, the
position was carefully examined. The experts said the weather
was likely to remain rough for an indefinite period. Only a
slight, temporary improvement was expected on the morning
of June 6th. Eisenhower, who was opposed to postponing the
invasion, decided to use this brief improvement. The invasion
was accordingly fixed for the early morning of June 6th, which
meant a delay of only twenty-four hours.

When Violette arrived at the country house at Sandy, she
learned that they were to fly in an American Liberator. An
American wireless operator named Jean-Claude Guiet was to
be the fourth member of their party. Guiet was only twenty
years old. Both his parents were French. He was born in
America and spoke French with not the slightest trace of
accent. He was tall and dark and quite good-looking. He held a
commission as second lieutenant in the United States Army,
but like the others he was not in uniform tonight. Violette had
on slacks and a leather jacket cut in the French style. The men
were in velvet trousers and jackets. All looked very French in
their appearance and their bearing. There was, of course, the
usual very thorough inspection of their clothes and the
contents of their pockets.

As they assembled for dinner and the introductions were made, Vera noticed again that Violette was the only girl going out on an operation. All the men in the room, of whom there were a large number, including swarms of Special Air Service boys, who were known as 'Jedburghs' (they were to land behind the lines in uniform) turned to look at her, some with admiring eyes, others with a certain misgiving, as though wondering what on earth this pretty little thing thought she was up to. Vera Atkins says: "There was great tension in the room that night. All the boys were going out on various operations. You could feel the jumpiness of their nerves. Astonishingly, Violette alone was perfectly calm and composed. I was very struck by the contrast."

In groups, as they were called, the others left their tables and set out by car for the aerodrome. Presently it was time for Staunton, Violette and their party to go too. They got up and, accompanied by Vera, made their way to Tempsford, with the blinds drawn as always so that even the ground staff should not see the secret agents.

The Liberator looked enormous after the tiny Lysander in which she flew out before. There was a crew of seven, all Americans in uniform. At the back of the plane where they were to sit behind the bomb racks (only tonight the plane carried not bombs, but containers filled with arms and explosives which were to be dropped with them), there was room just for the four, apart from the rear gunner and the dispatcher, whose task it would be to attend to their jump. These men too were Americans and in uniform.

The parachutes, which were not the ordinary service parachutes but very much larger ones made especially for airborne troops, since they were to be used as a means of transport and not as a lifebelt, had already been placed in the plane. Wearing their flying suits, with the zipper pockets full of weapons, rations, maps and compass, the four got in. Vera said her goodbyes. The engines were revved up and the plane began to throb. Just as it was taxiing along the runway a man came out with a message. It said that the weather ahead was very bad. A postponement to the next night was thereupon decided.

Frantic signals to the Liberator brought it to a halt and the four passengers got out again. Vera says: "On their faces one could see their acute disappointment. It was the most awful anticlimax – to say goodbye, to get into the plane, to be on the point of taking off and then to troop out again, get back into the car and drive back to the house."

In the common room at Hasell's Hall, some smiled, others exchanged whispers which might have been a little contemptuous, but Violette did not turn a hair. She walked straight past them, accepted a cigarette from Bob and had coffee, while Vera arranged accommodation for them for the night. The three men slept together in a room on the first floor. Violette had one to herself a few doors away.

Vera returned to town and rejoined them the next morning to make fresh plans for their departure. She found Violette engaged in a brisk game of ping-pong. "I have never seen her look more beautiful," says Vera. "She had on a pair of white marguerite earrings which she had bought in Paris. Her dress had a plunging neck-line. She wore no stockings, but just a pair of bright sandals. She made a really striking picture – her well-chiselled features, her high cheekbones, her eyes bright and lively, her hair so pretty: a lithe, girlish figure, young, strong and supple, she was bursting with health and pulsating with vitality, all of her just coiled energy." Again she was struck by her amazing calmness. "If she had any premonition about the future she certainly did not show it."

The three boys, with time on their hands for the rest of the day, borrowed a car and, taking Violette with them, motored, not into Bedford which was only ten miles away, but into Cambridge which was twice as far. There they had lunch and, though the day was grey and uninviting, spent the afternoon boating on the river. They came back in time for dinner and went through all the previous night's formalities of departure – the inspection of their clothes, the careful search of their pockets. Then they set out again for the airfield.

This time the plane took off. It was the night of the invasion, but they were unaware of it. Enclosed in the back of the plane they saw nothing, but the pilot and the others in front saw the greatest armada of ships ever known to history proceeding across the Channel. It was a breath-taking sight. All round them the air was thick with planes. Every aerodrome in Britain was in use that night. In an endless stream they flew, all going southward. Three airborne divisions were to follow them and seize objectives at Caen and elsewhere behind the enemy lines.

The Liberator flew high over the Normandy beaches, then, descending, made for the heart of France. It picked out the landmarks and located the landing-ground, which lay hidden amid the low hills to the south of Limoges. Again and again it circled the dark hills and fields looking for the small signalling lights, but the crew saw none. So no parachute drops could be made and the plane had to turn back. Once again they returned to the Tempsford and drove back to the club house. Wearily, for it was only an hour before dawn, they went up to their beds, the men together again in one room and Violette by herself in another.

At five o'clock in the morning the men were shaken out of their deep sleep and told to get up. "It's time, sir. Come on," called the batman.

"Why?" asked Bob.

"What time is it?" inquired Staunton.

Guiet, the American, just turned over and groaned.

"It's five o'clock, sir," said the batman.

At this pandemonium broke loose. "What the devil do you mean by waking us up at five in the morning?" … "What's the big idea anyway?" … "We're not wanted until the night."

The batman walked to the door and brought in the notice pinned to it. It stated: "Urgent. Please call us at 5 a.m. sharp, without fail – and see that we are up."

The boys jumped out of their beds in a fury. They deduced, rightly, that Violette had put the notice there. So they stormed into her room and shook her into wakefulness, then dragged her out of bed, poured a volley of angry oaths on her head and returned to their room.

At seven o'clock the boys were awakened again – this time by Violette herself. She had not gone back to sleep, but had dressed and gone down for breakfast. She went now from one bed to another, calling out in an excited voice, "The Invasion! We've landed. Come on, get up."

"Oh, for Heaven's sake …" groaned Staunton.

"Get back to your blasted bed and go to sleep," said Bob, throwing his pillow at her.

"It's true," she said. "Look!"

She had brought the morning papers and in a moment they were all poring over them, reading the thrilling details of D-Day.

They dressed speedily. They were anxious to be off. But they had of course to wait until the night.

Vera Atkins was already there when they got down. The reception committee near Limoges had got through during the small hours. German patrols, it appeared, had been on the prowl. In the circumstances, of course, no landing signals could be given.

Once again they went to Cambridge for the day. It was warm, though not sunny. They swam in the river, played tennis, and at about eleven o'clock that night, after still another inspection of their clothes and their pockets, once again they got into the Liberator and this time all was well.

The flight out took four hours. Violette and the three boys sat uncomfortably on the floor of the plane and played gin rummy. The American dispatcher marvelled at their composure. He beckoned to the rear gunner, who wrinkled his chin in confirmatory surprise. With Violette leading them in song, they raised their voices and yelled the tuneful chorus of *I'll Be Around*, which they had come to regard as their theme song. This convinced the Americans that the four were quite mad. At about two o'clock they helped themselves to rum and coffee from their flasks. An hour later they were over their objective.

The signalling lights were discernible quite clearly below. The dispatcher got the four into position. They put on their parachutes; the static line of each was clipped on to one of the rings attached to the walls of the plane. There was no hatch for them to jump through, but a hole had been cut for this purpose in the floor of the Liberator. The lid was lifted off this and

Violette, as the first to go, sat on the edge of the hole, with her legs dangling into the rushing wind below. For a moment she clung with her hands behind her, then she let go. The line drew taut and tugged open the 'chute. Staunton had by now taken her place, next came Bob, then Guiet. Slowly the four swung down to the earth. Taking another run above the field, the Liberator dropped the containers that held their suitcases, then four further containers, each containing Sten guns, Tommy guns, hand grenades, ammunition and explosives. The big plane then turned and made for home.

But instead of a reception committee of three, the four descending from the plane saw thirty men running across the field towards them. Remembering what nearly happened at Rouen and the cause of their turning back the night before, they wondered if it might be the Gestapo. Before they reached the earth they were seized by their feet, dragged down and covered with embraces and kisses. It was a most fervent welcome. No whispers here, they talked in their normal voices. Their torches were kept alight. A large car had been brought to take back the visitors and a lorry for the weapons and supplies.

They were now in the Maquis country. The people here had an arrogant confidence in their numbers and the utmost contempt for the Germans. They had been greatly heartened by the Allied landings in Normandy a few hours before, for they saw that the day of their deliverance was very near. They laughed and jested as they drove along the dark country roads, proclaiming proudly that there wasn't a German around for miles. The Germans as a rule kept clear of the Maquis areas: they found them difficult to control. But every now and again they made a sweep through this hilly, wooded country. Had they come again unexpectedly tonight there would undoubtedly have been a fight, for the reception committee had brought their guns with them. But the car and the lorry got through unchallenged to the little village of Sussac, where the visitors from England were to stay.

They were housed above a grocer's shop in the centre of the village. Once again Violette got a room to herself. The boys shared. The people did everything to make them comfortable.

131

There was plenty to eat in that country area, where cattle abounded. No ration cards were required. The Maquis ran the place their own way.

All voices in the house were hushed that night so that the guests should get a good night's rest and there was no question of getting up for breakfast. It was brought to their beds.

Chapter 16

The Ambush

Violette and her party arrived at Sussac in the small hours of the morning of June 7th, 1944. The Allied landings of twenty-four hours earlier had already established a foothold in Normandy and the Germans were rushing troops at reckless speed from all parts of France and Germany in order to dislodge them and drive them back into the sea. For months all the valiant endeavours of the French Section of SOE had been directed to the one end of preventing the German divisions from getting there now, or at any rate hampering and delaying their progress. Every group of Resistance workers behind the enemy lines had been allotted a specific task. Roads and bridges had to be blown up. Acts of sabotage had been arranged at factories and on the railways, at lock gates and at power stations. It was their purpose to cause the greatest possible destruction and to create a confusion that would distract and bewilder the enemy. Staunton's task in the Limoges area was to harness the Maquis most effectively to this same end.

He saw around him vast sections of Maquis, numbering 3,000 men in all. They were spread out across a hundred miles of country from Sussac northwards to Châteauroux. Through this great expanse of wooded land the Maquis roved as they pleased, save for occasional raids by detachments of heavily armed Germans. Two main roads to Normandy ran through this region – one from Toulouse, the other from Bordeaux. In its midst was the large industrial town of Limoges, which was completely under German control. The town was heavily guarded by German troops. There were road blocks at all points leading into the town and passes were required to enter and leave it. The Gestapo also had their headquarters for the area in Limoges.

Around Sussac were the Haute Vienne Maquis, numbering about 600. On learning of the Allied landings, the 200 gendarmes Pétain had in the area instantly joined forces with the Maquis. One of the chief figures in this group was a young man known by the code name of Anastasie. His real name was Jacques Dufour. He was tall, dark, heavy-browed and had sparkling eyes. He was born at Salon-la-Tour, a village not far from Sussac. For his daring exploits against them, the Germans had singled him out as 'the greatest bandit in the Limoges area'. They knew his real name and were determined to get him. A large sum of money was offered for Anastasie alive or dead and the Germans had even rounded up some Dufours who had a hotel in Salon-la-Tour, but were in no way related. To the south were the Corrèze Maquis, to the east the Creuse Maquis. Others stretched westward into the Dordogne.

For the most part these Maquis were farm hands and peasants. There was a sprinkling among them of Spaniards who had fought in the Civil War and refused to live under Franco, and just a handful of Poles. They dressed themselves in any uniform they could find or devise and looked like assorted figures out of a musical comedy. Some had gay jackets with gold epaulettes and wore feathers in their hats, others went about in khaki shorts or wore a khaki béret with their workaday corduroys.

Staunton says in his report: 'When I left London I was given to understand that I would find on arrival a very well-organised Maquis, strictly devoid of any political intrigues, which would constitute a very good basis for extending the circuit throughout the area. On arrival I did find a Maquis, which was roughly 600 strong, plus 200 French gendarmes who joined up on D-Day. But these men were strictly not trained, and were commanded by the most incapable people I have ever met, as was overwhelmingly proved by the fact that none of the D-Day targets had been attended to and that each time it took me several hours of discussions to get one small turnout, either to the railway or the telephone lines.'

The members of this force were indeed highly individualistic. When arms and explosives had been dropped to them in the past, instead of guarding them for co-ordinated and advantageous use on selected targets at the arranged signal, their one resolve had been to settle the war there and then by themselves. Buckling on their equipment and shouldering their rifles they set out in immediate quest of the enemy, provoked a battle and, having neither discipline nor a plan of campaign, suffered heavily in such engagements.

Staunton realised that his task was not going to be easy. In Rouen, starting from scratch, he had been able to recruit men and women who were willing to serve and to accept both discipline and training. Here he found disorganised bands who wanted only to go their own way. No doubt all the other groups of Maquis around here were similar in composition and attitude. At the head of them all, with the entire force of 3,000 nominally under his control, was a remote figure in Châteauroux. 'The Chief of this Maquis,' states Staunton in his report, 'a man who calls himself Colonel Charles, was by trade a saxophonist in a Bal Musette; a soldier of the second class with no war experience. He had been for Hector, Samuel and Anastasie (the leaders of the separate sections) their only contact with the neighbouring Maquis, which none of these leaders had every really visited, relying on Charles for their information.'

Staunton, who had come here with his team for the express purpose of organising and directing them, was resolved to get the entire Maquis force into immediate action. The German divisions were already on the march, so not a moment could be lost. Had Hitler listened to what Rommel had been urging for many months, these scattered divisions would already have been in the north, for that obviously was where they would be needed. But Hitler had an eye on the possibility of a landing in the South of France (which did indeed come not long after Normandy) and he felt that, by keeping his army dispersed, he would provide them with greater mobility and striking power. The most formidable of these divisions in the south was the

Das Reich SS Panzer division stationed at Toulouse and already on its way to Normandy to aid the hard-pressed German forces there. Soon it would be entering Maquis country. That was the time to strike and strike hard.

Staunton called an immediate council of action. Anastasie, as the chief of the local Maquis, listened attentively and expressed his readiness to co-operate to the full. What they had needed was a plan of operation. Now that the Allies had landed and things were moving so fast, the Maquis, he said, could be relied upon absolutely to strike at the enemy whenever and wherever required. He knew the country well – they all did. He would get his men into position at points of vantage with their explosive charges, their hand grenades and Tommy guns. "You can rely on us. The Das Reich division will never through," he said. The words, Staunton felt, had the swagger of the Maquis, but the spirit was there, he knew.

He thanked Anastasie. "That takes care of this territory. Now what about the others?"

"They will act too. I am sure of it," Anastasie said. "But we must take the plan to them – and it will have to be explained to them very carefully. We must send someone …" He glanced round the room.

"Violette will take it," said Staunton.

Anastasie looked at the girl. "Good," he said. "I will take her along to the Maquis nearest to us in the Corrèze."

"We need you here," said Staunton.

"But someone must give the girl the backing of our authority. They know me in the Corrèze. I will hand her over to Samuel, who is the leader there, and I shall be back in three – at most four hours."

"All right."

"She will explain the plan of operation – and Samuel will take her on personally, like me, to the next group of Maquis in the Creuse area. And so on, till in the end she gets to Colonel Charles at Châteauroux and tells him how we have decided to act."

"That sounds fine," said Staunton. "But remember there's a price on your head."

"Oh, I shall be all right. I'll be back in the afternoon," Anastasie assured him.

Turning to Violette, Staunton added: "Whatever happens we need Anastasie here. I want you to remember that. He is vital to our plans."

She nodded. "I understand."

Anastasie got busy at once. Things had to be got going quickly. On the morning of June 10th, that is to say three days after Violette's arrival, all was ready for her to start on her mission. The Maquis had collected in the preceding months vast stores of arms and explosives which were secreted in various dumps. They also had quite a number of motor-cars. Most of these were driven by wood fuel, but for this journey they brought out a large black Citroen and filled it up with petrol. The party assembled in the small square in Sussac in front of the grocer's where Violette, Staunton and the others lived. Violette was dressed in a light tailored suit, flat-heeled shoes and no stockings. She took a small suitcase with her and her Sten gun with eight magazines of ammunition. Anastasie, who had on his corduroys and a leather jacket, took his Tommy gun. It was a warm day, though the sun was obscured by clouds. Indeed the sky looked threatening, as though a storm might blow up at any minute.

The two got into the car and with a resounding cheer and a volley of good wishes set off at about half-past nine. Anastasie intended to take her to Pompadour, a charming little village about thirty miles away in the very heart of the Corrèze country. Pompadour is dominated by the fifteenth-century castle from which Antoinette Poisson, the mistress of Louis the Fifteenth, took her name.

The journey there was not expected to take much more than an hour. Almost all of it lay through narrow winding country lanes, not leafy but flanked by rocks and scrub. But they would have at some point to cross the main road from Toulouse to Normandy, and it was very possible that here they might encounter a Nazi division moving northward to Normandy with its tanks and fleet of lorries carrying supplies.

Anastasie had arranged to pick up on the way the son of a doctor who lived at La Croisille, about four miles from Sussac. The boy, who was not quite twelve years old, was going beyond Pompadour and was delighted to get a lift in the car, but brought his bicycle for the journey back. Violette and Anastasie helped him to rope it on to the side of the car. They placed it against the side Violette was sitting, so as to leave the door to the driver's seat clear. The boy got in at the back. The two in front kept their guns handy just in case there was trouble.

Anastasie decided to cross the main road at Salon-la-Tour.

He felt it would be an advantage to go through a village he knew so well. The people there, with whom he had lived since his childhood, would readily inform him of any activity by the Germans along the main road.

They sang, as they went, French songs that they all knew. As they passed under the railway bridge and approached the quiet sleepy little village of Salon-la-Tour, the storm clouds overhead descended in a heavy but brief downpour. Their lane swept westward and Anastasie pointed eagerly through the rain at the church, the huddle of white houses and the ivy-clad tower from which the village gets its name. "Look," he said, "I climbed up to the very top of that when I was nine and took lots of photographs with my small box camera."

They peered at the rain-slashed landscape on the right. "That's where I used to live. I'll take your right past it. On this other side, beyond the farms, is a little stream where my sister and I used to come and fish as children. We once saw a snake swallow a frog there."

The boy said: "It's going to be pretty slippery cycling back."

"Nonsense," said Anastasie. "Here's the sun trying to break through. This storm will be over in no time."

They went on towards the village street, beyond which lay the main road. Suddenly Anastasie pulled up. With lowered voice he said, "There's something behind that hedge – the further side – right in that field beyond."

"They're Germans," said Violette. "You can just see one of their caps."

The boy leapt out of the back of the car and ran into the nearest field. Anastasie got out too, Tommy gun in hand, and flung himself into a shallow ditch at the side of the road. Violette had to squeeze herself past the steering-wheel of the car. Seizing her Sten gun, she crossed the road to a tree. "Run," she called to the boy, but he was already scurrying fast across the fields.

Instantly the Germans began to shoot from the further side of the hedge. Violette turned her gun on them and blazed away too.

"Are you mad?" cried Anastasie. "Get down here. Come on. You haven't a dog's chance out there."

With a quick glance towards the boy, who was tearing towards home but was not yet out of sight, she sent a further burst of fire at the Germans.

"For Heaven's sake," shouted Anastasie. "Come down here."

"All right. All right," she cried. She crossed the lane, looked at the ditch. "That's not going to do much good," she said.

The Germans had by now emerged. There appeared to be about thirty of them. She saw that it was better to leave the lane and dash across the fields, where they might have a chance.

"This way," she said, prodding Anastasie with her foot.

Crouching, for the Germans had begun to fire again with their very rapid Schmeissers, Violette crept along the ditch to the wooden fence of a farmhouse and leapt over it. Anastasie followed instantly and they both flung themselves down on the wet earth. A woman tending her cows turned to see the cause of all this startling activity. She was caught in the German line of fire and was killed instantly.

The storm had by now blown over and the sun was out. Anastasie motioned to Violette, both rose quickly and ran forward. The bullets flew around them. One tore through Anastasie's jacket but did not even graze his skin. Both were running hard. Violette dashed out of the small field, crossed a narrow farm track and entered the yard of the adjoining farm, with Anastasie close at her heels. The farmer, who had come in to get a jacket because of the storm, gazed with alarm through his window at the fleeing figures. He saw Anastasie stuff a piece of paper into his mouth and, running to the further hedge, leap across it to the wide sloping meadows which swept down to the stream. Violette sped after him. By the time the Germans came up the figures were out of sight. Calling angrily to the farmer, they demanded the way the fugitives had gone. He said, being indoors and they tearing by so fast, he couldn't exactly tell, but thought they had gone that way. He pointed in the wrong direction.

By now still more Germans had come up. They were in fact the advance guard of the Das Reich SS Panzer division, sweeping the villages to make sure the division could proceed along the road unhindered. Four hundred strong, with armoured cars in support, they were clearing the surrounding countryside of Maquis assailants who, they felt, might be lying in wait with hand grenades and Tommy guns. Into the farmer's yard they poured in groups of twenty and fanned out, some taking the direction indicated, others tearing through the hedge to the meadows which sloped down to the stream. They were all heavily armed. Two armoured cars now appeared travelling along almost parallel farm tracks.

After some moments Violette and Anastasie, having waded through the stream, emerged, wet and out of breath, and could be seen dashing up the further slope towards a distant cornfield. Instantly the entire German advance guard dashed after them and the armoured cars turned and bounced along their tracks which, they all knew, converged at the far end.

Bullets began to fly fast now from the machineguns of the two armoured cars and the Schmeissers of the pursuing Germans. Violette received a slight flesh wound in her left arm. In a moment the two distant figures were lost in the cornfield amid the tall golden corn. They knew, since both had been well trained, that their progress would have to be zigzag or the bending corn would leave a revealing trail for the marksmen.

The German volleys continued, tearing into the corn.

"All right?" called Anastasie, who was a few yards in front.

"Fine," she called back.

"I've swallowed the code," he said. "So all's well."

Then suddenly Violette fell. Anastasie turned back in alarm and found her lying on the earth.

"It's nothing," she said. "Go on. I'm doing fine."

It was not a bullet, he found, that had brought her down, but her ankle, already damaged during her jumps at Ringway; it gave in the swift zigzagging to right and to left.

He picked her up in his arms, but she struggled hard to get free.

"Don't be a damned fool," she said. "We can't both be saved. You won't stand a chance if you're caught. Besides, you've work to do. Go on. Get out."

He carried her while she struggled. She beat hard against his shoulders with her fists, kicked and wriggled. The bullets still breezed past them and the chattering guns came ever nearer.

With a final desperate thrust Violette succeeded in bringing them both down. As they fell amid the corn, with her Sten gun clutched in her hands, she crawled to the edge of the cornfield, clamped a new magazine in and, crouching, limped her way to an apple tree.

She was an easy mark now. The bullets pinged and spat up spurts of earth. It was a miracle that she was not killed. She stood up, cocked her gun and began firing at the oncoming Germans.

"Run!" she called. "Run! For God's sake, make a run for it."

Some Germans were seen to fall, whether killed or wounded none could tell.

Anastasie saw that it was utterly hopeless now to go to her aid. "It's your last chance," she called again. "You can just make it." With that she pressed a fresh magazine into the gun and resumed her firing.

Anastasie rose, glanced about him like a hunted animal, and with a last burst at the Germans from his Tommy gun, ran out of the cornfield to the road at the top. The two armoured cars were not far away now. Both were making for the same point. There was just a chance that he would get there first.

Crouching, half dropping with exhaustion, he ran on and reached at last the railway bridge at the top and the small farmhouse beside it. At the corner of the road, by the bridge, lay a pile of logs. Anastasie decided to worm his way into their midst. They should with luck provide him with enough cover. From the window of the farmhouse the farmer watched with apprehension. At other windows stood his wife and two daughters. They knew Anastasie well. Both girls had been to school with him.

Quickly the girls came out. They piled the logs upon him and had just got him covered up when the first of the two armoured cars turned towards them. With the greatest alarm suddenly one of the girls saw that Anastasie's foot was exposed, so she sat down on it.

The Germans leapt down from the car and started their questioning. The girls admitted they had seen a man run by. He had leapt, they said, down to the railway lines.

Meanwhile, swarming across the fields, shot at continuously as they came, the Germans, numbering many hundreds, firing all the time, closed in on Violette. By now all the magazines of her Sten gun had been emptied. As they came to take her she fought them with immense strength for one so small. She kicked and struggled and struck at them with her fists, and bit their hands as they seized her. But she was no match for so many. Two Nazi soldiers eventually succeeded in pinioning her by the arms and half carried, half dragged her to the top, for she was utterly exhausted and in great pain.

They brought her, hot and dishevelled, to the heap of logs under which Anastasie was hidden and stood within a pace of him. The second armoured car now came up. A young officer, eyeing Violette with admiration, said: "I like your spirit. You put up a wonderful fight – right up to the end." Then, motioning to his men to let go her arms, he took out his cigarette-case, selected one for her and stuck it between her lips.

Some weeks before, while travelling with Germans in the train to Rouen, she had to appear to be affable in order to allay suspicion. But now the mask was off. She was no longer prepared to engage in an exchange of courtesies. She spat out the cigarette. Her eyes blazing with fury, she said: "You dirty cowards. You filthy German swine. I don't want your cigarettes—" and with that, leaning forward, she spat full in the young officer's face.

His eyes narrowed. Drawing his handkerchief, he wiped the spittle off his eyes and cheek. Then suddenly he threw his head back and laughed.

"All right," he said. "Take her away." He motioned towards the nearer armoured car. The two soldiers seized her and lifted her on to it. She refused the seat offered her.

The officer sprang on to the car himself. Hundreds of German soldiers meanwhile were swarming across the railway lines and beating the bushes in their search for Anastasie.

"We'll be back presently," the officer told the farmer, who was now standing at his door. "Get inside all of you. Not one of you must leave the house."

The girl sitting on Anastasie's foot hesitated for a moment. "Go on, get inside," the German officer commanded.

"All right, I'm going," she said casually.

She began to rise. With her body still covering the exposed foot, she waited until the armoured cars moved off. She heard Violette say: "Will you tell your men to let go my arms? I'd like to have one of my own cigarettes."

As the two armoured cars turned into the village street hundreds standing at their windows saw her go by in the leading car, with a cigarette between her lips, shouting death and damnation to the Germans. "Your fate is already sealed. The end is drawing near. It won't be long now. Then you swine will get your deserts in full."

Many Germans were seen to fall when they closed in on her, for they presented a wide semicircle which she raked with her gun. But none can tell the exact number, as the entire village remained behind closed doors for the rest of the day. No bodies were found. The Germans were not likely to leave their dead and wounded on the fields for the villagers to dispose of.

Anastasie lay under the logs for many hours. By adjusting one of the logs after the Germans left, the girls were able to keep the foot concealed until night fell. Then they came out and took him into the house. The farmer's wife had prepared a meal for him. He ate it ravenously. "If I live a hundred years," he said, "I shall never forget today." But as things turned out he was killed the following year in Indo-China. His body was brought home and lies in the little cemetery within sight of the fields across which he and Violette were pursued for close on two miles, fighting all the way.

In Salon-la-Tour even now they talk of that heroic day when *'la petite Anglaise'* held four hundred Germans of the Das Reich SS Panzer division at bay, with a complete disregard of all personal risk. It gave the boy they knew his chance to get away. Of the girl's real name they are unaware. They heard later that it was Corinne. That was the name entered in her forged papers. By it she is still known in the area.[1]

1. Later that afternoon another detachment of the Das Reich SS Panzer division, or it may even be the same detachment, went to Oradour-sur-Glane, not many miles further along the road, and massacred the entire village of 600 men, women and children to emphasise their determination to get through to Normandy. They never got through. It has been thought that Violette's shooting down of so many Germans may have been the cause of their savage revenge at Oradour.

Chapter 17

To the Rescue

Staunton learned of the ambush through the doctor's son. The boy returned to La Croisille very late in the afternoon, footsore and frightened. With his bicycle still roped to the abandoned car, which was found later riddled with bullets, the boy had to walk the nine miles to his home. The doctor, mounting his bicycle, took the news on to Sussac.

What the outcome was Staunton did not know. Neither Anastasie nor Violette had returned. Had they been killed or were they lying injured somewhere? He decided to set out at once and find out. His inquiries had to be made with the utmost discretion in case Violette and Anastasie were in hiding.

As he approached Salon-la-Tour late that night he was told that both had been taken prisoner. This report had been deliberately spread by the Germans, who said: "We caught the boy later in the woods. We've got him all right." Anastasie, as we know, was having a belated meal at the time behind locked doors, in the house of the farmer and his daughters. Nor did he venture to return to Sussac until three days later in case the Germans should still be on the look-out.

Staunton, however, got more definite news long before then. Early the next afternoon, two men came in from Limoges to see him. They said they belonged to the Resistance forces there. An English girl, believed to be a secret agent, had been brought in the night before by guards of the Das Reich SS Panzer division. She was lodged in Limoges jail and that morning they had seen her being taken by two guards to be questioned at the Gestapo headquarters. "A pretty girl," they said, "limping badly. But such dignity – and that look of utter contempt for her guards." If any help was required, they said, the Resistance in Limoges were ready to give it. It might even be possible to effect her rescue. Staunton asked about Anastasie. There was just the girl, they said.

Staunton decided that everything should be done to rescue her. It would have to be planned with the utmost care. The jail would have to be watched. The positioning of the guards, the times of her journey to Gestapo headquarters, for no doubt she would be taken there many times, would also have to be noted exactly. All this, he felt, might be better done by those who were already in Limoges, since new and unfamiliar faces would undoubtedly attract attention.

The men agreed and offered to undertake the work. It would be organised down to the last detail. Obviously it was going to involve a slow and very careful process of observation. Bob Mortier was deputed to keep in close touch with them and to rally such aid as might be required eventually from the outside for the carrying out of the rescue.

The jail at Limoges is a large sombre building with very high walls. It faces on to a wide paved square. Twice each day, at the hours of eleven in the morning and four in the afternoon, a little door, standing between two heavy ones, was opened and Violette was led out by two guards. They marched her, limping, across the square to the Gestapo headquarters down a street on the far side. This house, three stories high, stood right on the road. It was guarded of course. Violette was kept there for an hour, sometimes more, while the Gestapo colonel questioned her himself. Then she was led back to the jail. Thus there were four journeys in all every day, with only two guards in charge of her, though all around, in the streets and on the square, there were others to be reckoned with – German soldiers, either passing through or assembled for some purpose, or on guard outside certain buildings. The times of their assembly were noted, and checked on subsequent days to discern all possible variations. The hours at which the guards were changed were noted too. The passers-by, the shopkeepers, the residents, most of whom were of course French, but might be collaborators, had also to be taken into account. Patterns were detected in their coming and going. At some moments the streets were busy, at others they were comparatively deserted.

The watch revealed at the end of three days the precise hour at which the rescue could be made. Ten men would be needed, four to deal with the guards, the others to prevent any intervention. They would then seize Violette and place her in a motor-car, which, they felt, could be obtained quite easily: they had got cars before. But they would have to find a good one for this purpose, a car that was large and could travel fast. It was possible they would not be able to make their get-away in it, as all the exits from Limoges were heavily guarded. This, however, was where the men from Sussac could co-operate effectively.

When this report was brought to Staunton, he arranged that Bob should go into Limoges and work with the four men who were to deal with the guards. All would have to take along their Tommy guns in case anything went wrong. From Sussac a second car would be sent in with six armed men to deal with the guards at the town exit the moment they saw the rescue car approaching. Here, it was expected, they would have to fight it out.

The day selected for the rescue was Friday, June 16th – six days after Violette's capture. The hour was to be eleven o'clock in the forenoon. Carefully they went over all the details. Each man in each of the two groups rehearsed the role he was to play. Nothing was left to chance. Nothing could be allowed to go wrong.

Early on the Friday morning Bob went into Limoges with the faked pass of entry the Resistance men there had procured for him. Everything was ready. Just before ten o'clock the car they had earmarked for their purpose was stolen and held in readiness in a little-frequented side street. The four men who were to make the rescue with Bob checked their Tommy guns, saw that the spare magazines were accessible. They looked at their watches and waited.

Just before eleven o'clock they made their way towards the square in the car. They pulled up short of the square at a point from which the small prison gate through which Violette would be brought was fully in view.

The minute hand slowly approached the hour. Then the church clock began to strike eleven. It seemed to be a minute fast. Soon the hour was struck by other clocks in the town, some near, others distant and faintly audible. With their eyes on the jail door they waited. But there was no sign of it being opened.

The minutes passed. Something had apparently gone wrong. It was five past eleven. Then ten past eleven, and still there was no sign of Violette and her guards.

They waited until half past. Bob said: "Let's give it another half-hour. There may be a reason for the delay." But even at midday, as the clocks struck again, there was no sign of her.

It was learned later that Violette had been moved out of Limoges that very morning just before dawn. Where she had been taken nobody yet knew. On the day before she had made her four normal journeys to and from Gestapo headquarters. There had not been the slightest variation when they made their final check through.

Had their plot been discovered – or was it by the merest chance that she had been moved from Limoges at the eleventh hour? The acutest disappointment marked their faces. They escorted Bob to the town's exit, where the men in the second car were waiting and wondering what had happened.

Chapter 18

Into Germany

Violette was taken by road to Fresnes, the vast prison just outside Paris. It was a journey of over 200 miles. From the main
entrance on the road a long drive down an avenue of tall and
attractive trees takes one past a series of massive buildings on
the right, each with large heavy gates. At the third of these the
car pulled up. The gates were slowly swung back and, escorted
by her armed and uniformed Gestapo guards, she was led
through the yard into the section where the women prisoners
were kept. There was accommodation in that and the adjacent
male block for over 1,600 prisoners. In that summer of 1944 the
prison was full to overflowing. The men far outnumbered the
women and had five or even six prisoners in each cell, whereas
the women for the most part had a cell each to themselves.
Most of the prisoners were French, but others had been
brought in by the Germans from Jersey and Guernsey on
various charges and often on no charges at all but merely on
suspicion. Many were held as hostages, so that the threat of
their death might elicit information from relatives and friends
who were in hiding. The number of British prisoners here was
small and only a very few of these were secret agents.

What her fate there would be Violette had a fairly shrewd
idea. She had already sampled the severities of detention and it
was clear to her that her arrest had not been effected merely to
prevent her achieving a predesigned purpose, nor yet to punish
her for what she might already have accomplished, but to
extract from her certain vital information. At the Gestapo
headquarters in Limoges, to which she was taken twice each

day, the colonel of the Gestapo, seated in his office at his large desk, desired to know the plans in hand for the effective use of the Maquis in preventing the free movement of the German forces through that region. A large map of the area was produced. He wanted her to indicate the points selected for the blowing up of roads and railway lines, and for cutting communications. In view of the difficulties the Germans had already encountered in policing the area, and the added difficulties at this juncture because of the acute shortage of men, it was only by obtaining such information that time could be saved and much could be accomplished. He wanted to know where the vast supplies of arms were stored, what fields had been selected for parachute landings. He wanted to know the identity of the principals in the organisation and where they could be found (the Gestapo were, for example, aware of Anastasie's activities and had for a long time been trying to find him). He asked about the work on which she was herself engaged, the instructions she was carrying, the code used by the wireless operator, for each operator had his own individual code, and, as she had been taught to use the radio, it was felt that the code would be known to her or could be obtained by her. There was also the question of the expected landings in the South of France, in readiness for which ten German divisions had been kept in the south by Hitler. Had these landings been abandoned – or were they to be made now that these divisions were being moved to the north? It was a vital question and the Gestapo were convinced that a secret agent, strategically placed midway between north and south, must be able to supply the answer and they were determined to prise the information out of her if in fact she did possess it.

At first there was a show of affability and friendliness. She was told by her Gestapo inquisitor that it was not their purpose to torture or even to punish her. All they wanted were answers to a few simple questions. She did not deny that she knew some at least of the answers. She merely refused to answer any of the questions. There then followed a protracted process of persuasion. It began quite calmly with an endeavour to prove that the people for whom she worked did not care what became of her, whether she survived or was executed. Their one desire had been to use her and, if she failed, to use in her place someone else. "They will not lift a finger to save you or help you. We, on the other hand, want to – and can." She did not know that at that moment plans were in hand for her rescue, nor would it have mattered if she had. She realised that her work had now taken on a completely new form. It was only by her silence now that she could make her greatest contribution to the cause. No matter what pain and suffering she might be called upon to endure, that silence would have to be maintained and she prayed that she would be strong enough for the ordeal when it came. "I must not show any fear," she said again and again to herself, and in her heart she knew none; for she had been aware all along of the price she might one day be called upon to pay. Her face was composed as she listened to the colonel's soft-voiced expressions of concern for her and his desire to help her. "Of course you Germans always are most considerate and kind to your enemies," she said with a mocking smile.

"Of course." It was then that she laughed.

This angered the colonel. He instantly ordered the guards to take her back to the jail.

Some hours later she was brought again before him and the persuasion went on.

"It is only a question of time," he said, "before we find out everything – yes, everything we want to know. I want you to save us this loss of time, and in return I will guarantee you your life and the lives of your friends. All those whose names you give me …"

She merely exploded with laughter. "What do you take me for? A half-wit?"

A day or two later he appeared to have learned one or two things about her.

"You are really French," he said, "and you should give a thought to the fate of your own people. Your husband, who was also a Frenchman, very foolishly allowed himself to be used by the English. What good did it do him – or France? He lost his life, as you will lose yours if you persist in remaining silent. He could have lived in peace with us. There is peace between Marshal Pétain and ourselves. We arranged a most generous peace. But your husband is dead – just one of many thousands who have been too blind to see things clearly. You have been very, very stupid.

"You have a child, I believe – haven't you? What do you think is going to become of your child if we shoot you? Mind you, I don't want to shoot you. I am anxious to help you. I want to see you get back to your home…"

"You do talk a lot of silly rot," she interrupted. "I'll tell you nothing – nothing. Can't you get that into your head? No matter what you do, it won't make any difference. I despise you – I despise the whole lot of you." With the agility of a young animal she took a quick menacing pace towards him, but the two guards sprang forward and seized her to prevent whatever mischief she had in mind.

"Take her away," said the colonel.

She had noticed that he had made no mention at all of her earlier mission to Rouen and Le Havre. It seemed obvious that he did not know of it. She was puzzled how he had learned of her marriage. Was it just a shot in the dark?

The next morning at eleven she was brought in again. And so it went on until in anger he ordered her removal to Fresnes. "We shall see if that will bring you to your senses," he said.

"It isn't my senses you should be concerned about, but your own. In a very short time the tables will be turned. Then you will be standing here and one of our men will be seated in that chair."

That indeed happened much sooner than she anticipated, though not entirely as she foresaw it. She knew, of course, that Anastasie had completed all his plans for harrying and impeding the movement of German troops before they set out together on their fateful journey. These plans had since been put into operation. The messages she was to deliver were taken on by others and the work was thus spread out over the entire Maquis area. Railway lines were torn out. Bridges were destroyed. The road was blown up at many points and as fast as one section was repaired the Maquis speedily blew up another. Ambushes were constantly operated. If the German troops survived one, a little further on they ran into another. The Germans threatened to shoot hostages, but that did not deter the Maquis. "We piled up in a deep cutting two kilometres north of Salon-la-Tour," Staunton states in his report, "two successive passenger trains. This produced an effective block for six weeks, the Germans being short of heavy cranes." At the same time the Maquis in the Corrèze piled several tons of rock on the line between Uzerche and Brive. As a result of all this the Das Reich SS Panzer division never reached Normandy. The fighting there was over before it could get through.

Of all these operations Jean-Claude Guiet, the American wireless operator attached to Staunton, kept London fully informed and, through him, fresh directions were constantly being received with regard to work that had still to be done.

These developments occurred for the most part while Violette was at Fresnes; they brought about a complete reversal of the position at Gestapo headquarters in Limoges, as will presently be revealed.

With her suitcase left in the car at Salon-la-Tour, she was without any change of clothing and not even her handbag – no comb or toothbrush, not a pair of stockings or a handkerchief. At the jail at Limoges they brought her two coarse garments to wear as underclothes and for the rest she had to make do during the six days she was there with what she had on. On arrival at Fresnes, after her name had been entered in the office off the hall, she was led away by an SS wardress in grey, through a long underground passage, then up an iron staircase off which ran tier upon tier of corridors, caged in with iron bars, until they reached a cell on the fourth floor.

It was a small, dark cell, measuring about twelve feet by eight. The plaster was peeling off the walls, leaving horrible scars. On the wall opposite the door was a dirty window made up of small panes of frosted glass and heavily barred on the outside. The window could not be opened, for the handle had been wrenched off, but fortunately some of the panes had been smashed. The bed, a very rough and rusty iron frame, was folded against the wall. There was a lumpy palliasse to serve as mattress when the bed was let down. A rickety chair was the only other piece of furniture. There was a lavatory seat by the door with a cold-water tap above it.

When she looked at the walls later Violette was able to discern numerous scratches, made with the fingernail or a hairpin. They were mostly dates, a phrase or two from a prayer and a few angry words and curses. She had been brought up to believe that being sent to prison was a disgrace that one would never be able to live down; but here, as at Limoges, she felt a little proud that she could still make her personal contribution to the war. So far the Germans had extracted no information from her. Would she be able to hold out – and for how long, she wondered.

As night began to fall she heard raised voices, mostly the voices of the women in the cells around. In the gathering gloom of the unlighted cells, these voices seemed to bring an unseen companionship; for together, as one led and the rest joined in, some voices delightfully musical, others cracked and tuneless, they sang the old songs of France and of other countries. At intervals, rising above the singing, came harsh, defiant curses and cries of *'Courage, mon vieux'* and *'Vive de Gaulle"* and *'Vive Churchill'*. Curses, vile and bitter curses, were heaped too upon the heads of Laval and Pétain, who were regarded as primarily responsible for the sufferings they were all enduring. Violette, who joined vehemently in these curses, would have derived some comfort had she known that in a very few months both Laval and Pétain would be occupying cells in this very prison.

A trolley trundling on rails along the corridor brought them their food. In the evenings it was cabbage soup with a few beans in it. This was brought in a wooden tub and, as the prison was very crowded and the wardresses did not want to waste time opening doors, they poured the soup through the peep-hole into a small rusty tin bowl on a ledge on the inside. Bread was restricted to 100 grammes a day. Sometimes a piece of cheese was served, usually it was unfit for human consumption. A thin finger of margarine appeared occasionally and even, more rarely one got a solitary sausage, made, one found, of meat and bread salvaged from a bombed warehouse with bits of brick still in it. Not much nourishment could be obtained from such a diet and Violette, like the other prisoners there, was always very hungry.

For what purpose she had been brought to Fresnes was revealed a day later when the wardress opened the door and led her away. She was taken along the metalled corridor, down many flights of stairs, through the underground passage again, and out into the front yard. Here a Black Maria was waiting to take her into Paris.

As the van was windowless, save for a small grille in the back door, she caught only fleeting glimpses of the streets through which only a few weeks before she had roamed in freedom. She knew where she was being taken, for they had talked of it in England. It was to the house in the Avenue Foch where the Gestapo did their harsher questioning, aided by the persuasive refinements of torture. So it had come – the ordeal that had been constantly at the back of her mind. Urged by curiosity, and perhaps even awe, she had visited the Avenue Foch when she was last here and, with a swift glance at No. 84, she had walked quickly on.

Now, as the Black Maria swept along the Paris streets, she saw people seated in groups at the little round tables of the pavement cafés. The van turned into the Avenue Foch, one of the most attractive streets in all Paris, running from the Arc de Triomphe to the Bois. Gardens flanked it on both sides. The van coursed along an inner track which gave access to the houses and pulled up at No. 84. The guards swung back the gate, and she alighted in the sombre covered entrance to the house.

It was not at all like the Gestapo headquarters at Limoges. Once a private residence, it was almost palatial. A wide staircase led to five floors, each with many rooms that were used by the Gestapo for questioning and for torture. Her inquisitor was not in uniform. He was young, good-looking and rather dandified. His manner was calm, polite and assured. He had been carefully selected and trained for the work he was to do, just as she had been for hers. And he was determined to get the information he sought.

At that first interview he was unsuccessful. He was patient on that occasion, but when she was brought before him again the next day, after a bleak and uneasy night in her cell at Fresnes with a short, sharp volley from a firing squad under her window early in the morning (staged possibly for her benefit), she realised that today he meant to get down to business. This was confirmed by the presence in the room of a second man. The moment she sat down the man came up and stood by her chair. As the questioning proceeded and she still proved recalcitrant, implements of torture were produced and each was held up before her. The inquisitor said: "Will you answer now?" and, just as defiantly as when she was a child, she replied: "I won't. I *won't*" The young German then gave the sign. There followed the most atrocious torture.

She winced and bit her lips. Her face was contorted in her horrible agony. But still, though hardly able to move her lips, her eyes unable now to flash their fire, she repeated, almost inaudibly: "I won't. I *won't.*"

After a time the man said: "All right, take her away." Then, turning to her, he added: "I have given you your chance. As you won't speak, there seems to be nothing left now but the firing squad."

She refused to be assisted from the room. "Don't touch me," she said as, limping, she walked from the room.

She was in an agony for many days. Tossing amid constant discomfort and pain, her mind groped for precious memories from the past. The soothing hands of Etienne were on her brow, she heard again his whispered words of comfort, and she drew to her breast the warm, tender caresses of her child.

She did not know when she would be taken again to the Avenue Foch, or on which morning it would be her turn to face the firing squad. But, mingled with the dread and the suffering, was a feeling of elation. She had said nothing. By not one word had she betrayed what she knew. Mentally she felt invigorated, and she thanked God that she had been strong.

She wondered if her friends in Sussac knew where she was. They had, of course, heard that she had been taken to Fresnes and they were aware what the Fresnes prisoners had to undergo at the Avenue Bosche, as they called it. But Paris was too far away for any further attempt at rescue. Besides, they had important work in hand, which they had been undertaking with efficiency and dispatch. On June 25th, that is to say a fortnight after her capture and only a few days following her torture, the first parachute drop ever made by daylight during the war was made near Sussac. It was on a formidable scale. A force of eighty-six Flying Fortresses came over attended by many Lightnings and Mustangs. They dropped 864 containers filled with supplies – weapons, ammunition, hand grenades, explosives, stores, petrol and even money. It took 300 Maquis three days to carry these supplies away. Thirty lorries were used. All the roads on this journey were guarded by Maquis, who even put up road blocks at vital points to prevent the Germans getting in.

The effect of this vast daylight operation was electrifying. Seeing the planes come over in such great numbers, the entire countryside rushed into the fields to witness the unforgettable scene. As the hundreds of parachutes descended in successive waves, cheer upon cheer rose to greet them. There was the wildest jubilation. The people began to sing and sang while they loaded the trucks and took the supplies home. The few hundred Maquis of the Haute Vienne swelled overnight to well over 3,000.

Of all this Violette, of course, knew nothing. The Germans did not send for her again. At the Avenue Foch they were anxious and short tempered. Too much was happening in swift and startling succession in every direction. Much of Normandy was in Allied hands by the end of June. The Maquis were rising everywhere as fresh supplies reached them. In July an American assault group, comprising thirty men, all in uniform, was dropped by night in the Sussac area. Bob Mortier, who was in charge of the reception committee, had met some of the parachuted men in London. They included two English officers, Captain Bissett and Captain Ted Fraser, who had been conducting officers for the French Section of SOE. Shortly afterwards, in the next parachuted batch, came Major de Guelis, who had been responsible for recruiting Bob Mortier in North Africa and sending him to Buckmaster in London; and young André Simon, son of the famous wine connoisseur. A third group followed composed entirely of French Special Air Service officers. Together they totalled just on a hundred. Arriving in such numbers, these highly trained officers both strengthened and heartened the Maquis. Staunton and Bob and Guiet unpacked the uniforms they had brought with them and wore them always thereafter. It was sad, they felt, that Violette's uniform had to remain in the suitcase she left behind above the grocer's shop at Sussac.

She spent her birthday in bed in the most acute pain. It was her twenty-third birthday and the last she was to know. Etienne had been dead for two years: it was three years since their last meeting. All through July she remained at Fresnes, the pain easing, her spirits rising, for, despite German efforts to withhold all news of these tremendous developments, some of it inevitably percolated through. Women tapped it out in the Morse code on the walls of their cells to tell their neighbours. In the evenings, as darkness fell, there was a greater lustiness in their singing. Violette led them in the singing of the British National Anthem. But only two voices joined hers, the others apparently did not know the words, but made a valiant effort at *la-la*-ing to give support. It suggested, of course, that there were only two other women from England in the prison at Fresnes.

The Allies landed in the South of France in the middle of August. They did not drive north in the direction of the Maquis of the Haute Vienne, but turned eastward and pursued the Germans up the Rhone Valley into Germany. Staunton and his group made their own swift moves. With what was now quite a large and well-disciplined force they harried the Germans to right and to left, giving them no respite, and on August 20th they entered Limoges. General Gleiniger, commanding the German forces there, refused at first to surrender. On Staunton pointing out that the town was

158

surrounded by a force 20,000 strong, with reinforcements on the way, Gleiniger signed the surrender. His troops laid down their arms and were moved into a former prison camp for Jews.[1]

The next morning, Staunton, Bob and Guiet moved into the Gestapo headquarters. In the room in which Violette was so persistently questioned only two months before, Staunton now sat in the colonel's chair. The Gestapo, shirking the consequences of the altered situation, had already fled. Staunton was not, however, concerned with questioning and threatening. He had a bar set up at one end of the room, gaudily arrayed with bottles of whisky and the gay liqueurs of France. Here, while they planned their next moves, they were able in that blazing summer of 1944 to assuage their thirsts and to drink a toast to the courage, devotion and steadfastness of Violette.

Early in August there was bewilderment and alarm among the Germans in Paris, for the Third United States Army, under General Paton, and the Free French Forces led by General Leclerc, were marching steadily on the capital. Nothing the Germans could do could stop them. Each day the panic grew. Orders came suddenly for the removal of certain specially selected prisoners from Fresnes to Germany as the Gestapo did not want them 'to become available' to the advancing Allies.

On the morning of August 8th, that is to say seven and a half weeks after being brought to Fresnes, Violette was taken through the underground passage into the prison yard. There she saw three small coaches waiting. One of them was just moving off with a batch of male prisoners. The second, also containing men, was not yet full. She thought she saw in it someone she knew. He raised his hand in greeting and she realised that it was Harry Peulevé. For months she had been seeking him in London. It was strange that they should have

---

1. The Supreme Allied Commander, General Eisenhower, has recorded: 'Thanks to the underground movement the liberation of France was accelerated by some six months.'

been so near to each other in Fresnes. In the third coach there were fewer than a dozen girls. Harry called to her as his coach drove out. They could not speak, but there was the hope that they might meet if they happened to be travelling by the same train.

Harry was in London when the war broke out. He instantly joined the Territorials, served in France with the British Expeditionary Force and was evacuated at Dunkirk. He was a secret agent when he first met Violette at the Studio Club and had already been to France on a mission. She was working at the aircraft factory in Morden at the time. Etienne had been dead for nearly eight months, but Violette did not yet know it. A few weeks later, on learning the sad news about Etienne, Violette was herself to become a member of Harry's section of SOE and, though the girl who introduced them at the club that night had apparently a hand in getting Violette's name sent to the War Office, it was not until after the war that she revealed this to Harry. This girl, widow of a Battle of Britain pilot, who could not serve herself because she was an Italian by birth, wrote to say of Violette that she was 'an extremely suitable candidate for work in France as a secret agent.' At their next encounter in the Piccadilly underground, Harry saw that Violette had on the uniform of a FANY. They went about a great deal together after that and some thought a romance might be developing. The last time they saw each other was early in 1944. They were with a large party at the Astor Club. Two nights later he left. He was dropped not far from where Violette was herself to come not many months later, for he was with the Maquis in the Corrèze area, only a few miles from Salon-la-Tour. Harry was arrested in March 1944, Violette in June; and both had been for many weeks in adjoining blocks at Fresnes.

As each coach left the prison yard parcels of food, enough to last for two days, were handed to the prisoners by the Red Cross. Those who had suitcases were given them now. Violette had only a bundle containing the few garments given her in the prison at Limoges. No prisoner got back either jewellery or money, even their watches and rings were withheld. Etienne's engagement ring, which Violette had hoped to convert into cash when in a tight corner, she never saw again.

The men handcuffed in pairs, but the girls unfettered, they were taken to the Gare de l'Est and put into the train for Germany. It was not a long train. For the prisoners there was just one coach, which had been tacked on at the end. The other carriages were filled with German wounded. There was also an anti-aircraft gun in case of a raid.

The prisoners' coach had a lavatory and next to it a third-class compartment in which the girls were placed. Beyond that was what looked like two horse-boxes with stout iron doors that worked like lift gates and were kept shut to prevent access to the corridor. They had been formed by removing the seats from two compartments. Guards paraded the corridor and had a small compartment of their own to sit in just beyond the horse-boxes.

The girls were no sooner ushered into their compartment than they were chained by the ankles, in pairs. This was to prevent escape since there was no grille on their door.

After a wait at the station of many hours, during which, despite their efforts, Violette and Harry were unable to get to each other, the train started at last very late in the afternoon. It was obvious that the men would not be able to sleep, for there were nineteen of them in one section and eighteen in the other, with barely enough room to stand. Yeo-Thomas, known now as 'The White Rabbit', who was a director of Molyneux in Paris before the war, took charge, as the senior ranking officer among the prisoners. He arranged that they should take it in turn to lie down during the night, as only two pairs could do this at a time while the rest stood. It was a stiflingly hot August night and the men suffered the acutest discomfort. The women, though crowded closely together, at any rate had seats. Violette met now the two other Englishwomen at Fresnes. They were Denise Bloch and Lillian Rolfe; both had been wireless operators in the French Section of SOE. Lillian, who came from Horsell, near Woking, in Surrey, was tall and dark, with attractive brown eyes. She had a French mother and had been brought up in Brazil. Denise, broad-shouldered and blonde, had escaped from France during the Occupation. These three were to remain together through many ghastly and tragic developments.

In the morning, after a restless and exhausting night, the men were taken to the lavatory in pairs, still handcuffed together. The guard stood by the open door all the time. No further visits were allowed. As the day wore on the heat became increasingly intense. By the afternoon it was unbearable. The water, supplied in bottles by the Red Cross, had all been drunk during the night. The men kept clamouring for something to quench their raging thirst. They begged the guards to bring them just a glassful, but the guards ignored their pleas.

There were recurrent alarms that British planes had been seen overhead and there was a great fear that the train might be attacked. Near Chalons-sur-Marne, having come only eighty miles in twenty-two hours, these fears materialised. Two RAF planes bombed the train. There was a thundering explosion. Many windows were smashed. The train shuddered and came to a halt. In a panic the guards locked the doors of the coach and ran out into the fields where they took refuge in ditches. A machinegun was mounted on a small mound and trained on the carriage so that none might try to escape. The anti-aircraft gun got into action. Flying very low, the RAF planes dropped more bombs and then opened fire with their machineguns. The roof of one of the carriages was split open and the prisoners heard the screams of the wounded and the dying.

The women had begun to cheer at the start of the attack, but the men, imprisoned in confined spaces behind the locked grilles, were possessed by the fear that, if an incendiary hit their coach, there could for them be no escape and they would all inevitably be burned to death. There were Belgians and Frenchmen among them and some of them got hysterical. Unable to throw themselves down on the floor, they threw themselves on top of each other. A few were frothing at the mouth. Yeo-Thomas says: "We all felt deeply ashamed when we saw Violette Szabo, while the raid was still on, come crawling along the corridor towards us with a jug of water which she had filled in the lavatory. She handed it to us through the iron bars. With her, crawling too, came the girl to whose ankle she was chained."

This act of mercy made an unforgettable impression on all. She spoke words of comfort, jested, went back with the jug to fill it again and again. "My God, that girl had guts," says Yeo-Thomas. "I shall never forget that moment," says Harry Peulevé, "I felt very proud that I knew her. She looked so pretty, despite her shabby clothes and her lack of make-up – and she was full of good cheer. I have never under any circumstances known her to be depressed or moody."

When the planes departed and the guards returned, it was found that seventeen Germans had been killed. The raid was successful, says Yeo-Thomas. Either the engine or the track must have been damaged, for the train was unable to proceed. After a very long wait the prisoners were led out of their coach by the guards and put into two trucks requisitioned from farmers.

The trucks took them on to Metz, once regarded as a vital sector of the Maginot Line. Here they spent the night in the stables attached to the barracks. Straw had been spread out in the loose boxes. The men, also chained in pairs now, were given the stalls on the right, the women were separated from them by a narrow alleyway along which flowed the stable drain. The guards threatened to shoot if any attempt was made to cross from one side to the other. None the less, as the night advanced, some of the men and women crawled towards each other and talked across the drain until dawn. Peulevé says: "Violette and I talked all through the night. Her voice, as always, was so sweet and soothing, one could listen to it for hours. We spoke of old times and we told each other our experiences in France. Bit by bit everything was unfolded – her life in Fresnes, her interviews at the Avenue Foch. But either through modesty or a sense of delicacy, since some of the tortures were too intimate in their application or perhaps because she did not wish to live again through the pain of it, she spoke hardly at all about the tortures she had been made to suffer. She was in a cheerful mood. Her spirits were high. She was confident of victory and was resolved on escaping no matter where they took her."

Thus, in the darkness, with each chained by the ankle to another and the drain between them, they had their last romantic interchanges, with their hopes and dreams unvoiced but no doubt shared.

The journey to the German frontier took the best part of a week. They were taken from Metz to the Gestapo headquarters at Strasbourg and then northward to Saarbrücken. Here the women were detached from the rest of the party and sent off to Ravensbrück.

Chapter 19

Ravensbrück

Violette arrived at Ravensbrück in the last week of August 1944. She had been brought across the greater part of Germany, for Ravensbrück stood on the lakes of Mecklenburg, about fifty miles to the north of Berlin.

It was the largest prison camp in Europe, indeed the largest prison for women the world had ever known. When it was first built on these swampy marshlands in 1939, it was designed to accommodate 7,000 women prisoners in groups of huts. But the number of women grew as the war progressed. By the time Violette arrived, there were 40,000 women, crowded together in large huts and sleeping often six in a bunk on straw. In all nearly 120,000 prisoners are known to have entered it. Of these fewer than 12,000 were alive when the Russian advance overshot the camp and gave them their freedom. The Soviet soldiers, tough and hard-bitten, were appalled by the pitiful condition in which they found the survivors.

The place was like a walled town, with electrified barbed wire above the high walls. Inside, around and beyond a central square, were groups of huts, separated by rough rutted roads. The beds were built in double-tiered bunks, with only one blanket for three or four women to share. There were workshops, laundries, large rooms in which the prisoners were made to weave or to sew, and a very small compound for a handful of male prisoners. At one corner, near the crematorium (which was just outside the walls) was the Bunker or *Zellenbau*. Here women, and men too, had to undergo solitary confinement. Few in the Bunker escaped the firing squad or the gas chamber.

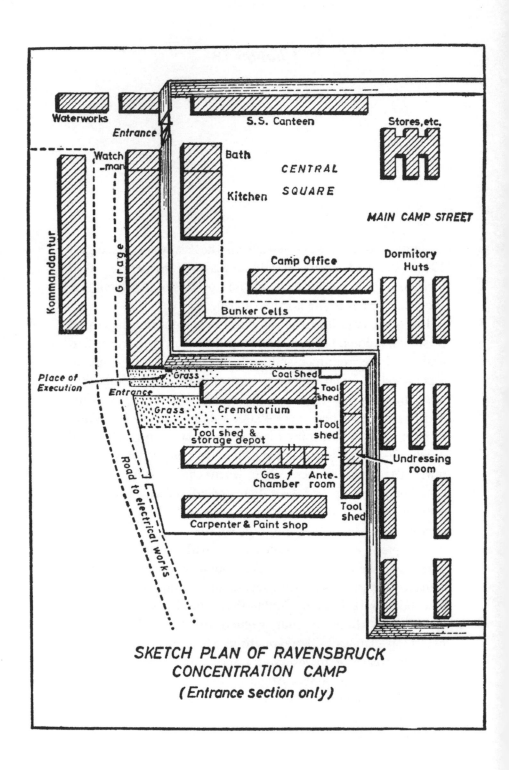

**SKETCH PLAN OF RAVENSBRUCK
CONCENTRATION CAMP**
(Entrance section only)

The heavy mortality suffered by the prisoners was attributed to exposure, overcrowding, lack of sanitation, inadequacy of clothing, undernourishment and overwork. They had only a single cotton garment and two thin slips of underwear, even in the bitterest winter when snow lay thick all round. They suffered also constant ill-treatment and brutality from the guards. The Kapo, or camp police, were constantly on the look-out for breaches of discipline or refusal to work, and the punishments inflicted were readily carried out by some of the internees in return for extra rations. All day long carts went round picking up the dead and the dying. It was later admitted by the officials that between sixty and seventy died every day.

As the truck bringing Violette and the other women from Fresnes drove in through the massive gate, heavily built female guards in jack-boots came up flourishing their whips. Each prisoner as she alighted was struck, punched, kicked and slapped by the guards. It was a way of getting them acclimatised.

They were led through a porch on the right into a large room. Here they were told to take off all their clothes. Some did it shyly, others with an air of indifference. Soon after the prisoners were undressed the doors opened and two men in uniform strode in. This caused considerable embarrassment to most of the women. The men, it appeared, were a doctor and a dentist, and the women were made to stand in a row for the inspection. In the ceiling were a large number of sprinklers of the shower type. They were now turned on. Water poured down on to the new arrivals and after this superficial bath, they were taken to a pile of clothes and told to help themselves. The garments they arrived in were taken away and never returned. The pile to which they were led contained shabby dresses, underwear of sorts, and an assortment of wooden shoes. Violette had already lost all her own things, so it did not matter much to her. Through all these unpleasant preliminaries her mind, trained to take in everything, was already seeking a possible mode of escape. Had anyone ever got out of Ravensbrück, she wondered? It did not seem at all possible, but a way might be found – would have to be found. On that she was resolved.

When they were assigned to their huts she was glad to see that Lillian Rolfe and Denise Bloch were to be with her. They contrived indeed, after much argument with the other women, to share the same bunk with two others.

Of the women in the camp by far the greatest number were Russians and Poles. There were Czechs too and Danes, Norwegians, Belgians, Dutch, French and even Germans. Only twelve were English and fourteen American. They could not all be spies or secret agents. Had they all fallen foul of the Gestapo that they should be confined in a prison under such strict surveillance? The fact is that the bulk of them were there for no crime that they were aware of committing. Most of them, taken away when the German armies invaded their countries, had been placed in work camps and, through insubordination or defiance, or because of malicious tales told against them by their fellow prisoners, had been sent on here. Others had been brought here in order to punish their husbands or lovers or fathers, for it was a way of getting the men to talk, but whether the men did or not the women remained, for there was work to be done here. Every morning they were roused at five o'clock – in the summer it was as early as three-thirty – and assembled in the central square, where a roll-call was taken. This lasted often as long as two hours, the prisoners standing at attention all the time. They were then formed into work-parties and marched away, some to weave, others to spin, others to work in one of the factories for textiles or electrical equipment, or to load and unload lorries, or to make roads. The duties varied from day to day according to their physical fitness. At all these tasks overseers stood by them and urged them on with whips. If their output lagged they received the most cruel punishments. They were kept at work for close on eleven hours and suffered inevitably immense strain on their inadequate diet.

The food, for which they had to queue, consisted of a bowl of artificial coffee in the morning, some soup made of cabbages or potatoes at midday, and the same soup again in the evening. They received in addition a small piece of bread, approximating to about one-tenth of a loaf, which had to last through the day. That was all. From time to time Red Cross parcels arrived for the prisoners, which they were made to sign for, but the parcels were taken away by the camp officials and enjoyed by their families in their own homes. To divert themselves the guards would throw bits of bread that had gone mouldy into the midst of the prisoners for the sheer pleasure of seeing them fight for it like demented animals.

The entire camp was infested by vermin. The smell in many parts, caused through lack of sanitation, was quite unbearable. Savage dogs, trained to attack the prisoners, were set upon them from time to time and there were appalling cases of suffering from dog bites.

Violette realised that her chance of escape was exceedingly slim. Chosen because of her still robust health to work on the roads, she felt that this might provide her with an opportunity. As she trooped out with the gang to the section outside the walls at which they were to work, her active mind sought the best means of breaking away. Each day the plan advanced a stage further and at last she took it. But she did not get far. The guards were too vigilant. She was led before the commandant, the inhuman Fritz Sühren, who ordered her to be beaten cruelly. A few days later she and her two friends were sent to Torgau. Violette had been in Ravensbrück in all only two and a half weeks.

Torgau lies about half-way between Berlin and Leipzig and is close on 120 miles to the south of Ravensbrück. This small town was before the war the centre of the accordion industry. Most of the accordions that the Germans sang to in their beer halls and their homes were made here. But the factories had been taken over for war work and were now making precision tools or serving the needs of the Luftwaffe.

Violette found conditions at Torgau infinitely better than at Ravensbrück. For one thing, where she was lodged it was not so much a prison as a work camp. The huts were less congested and the food a little more palatable. The guards, though numerous and heavily armed, were far less brutal. The work she was set to do was in an aircraft factory and not unlike the work she had been doing at Morden before she became a secret agent.

Here the chances of escape seemed a little easier. She intended this time to plan it with the utmost care and to obtain, if possible, the co-operation of people she could trust. It would of course, she realised, take a great deal of time. Always cheerful, ever ready with a jest, her light-hearted affability won her the regard of many of the other prisoners. Some of the men slipped her some cigarettes and chocolates that they had managed to get smuggled in, and with their aid she contrived to send off, for the first time since her capture at Salon-la-Tour, a brief message to her parents.

Mrs Bushell had been informed of course by Buckmaster that Violette had been arrested by the Gestapo. This news reached her in August when Violette was already on her way to Ravensbrück. Now, at the end of September, Violette managed to send a card. It took many months to reach Brixton. Mr and Mrs Bushell did not in fact get it until January 10th, 1945, that is to say more than seven months after Violette's departure from England on her second mission and five months after they had been told that she was a prisoner. The card did not say much. It was in fact somewhat puzzling. For one thing it did not bear her signature, but was signed with the single word 'Petit', as though it were a masculine surname. It might of course also have meant 'The Little One', but it was not in its feminine form. The card read: 'Dear Godfather, I am pleased to say that I am well. It is a long time since I wrote. Glad to hear from you. Happy to say I have met Violette. She is well and wishing for the war to end, as I do – Petit.'

At any rate it indicated that their daughter was well and that it was at her direction that the message had been sent. The card bore no address, but just the single word 'Leipzig', which is about fifty miles from Torgau.

Violette, meanwhile, was working ceaselessly on her plan of escape. A man in the precision tools section fashioned most cunningly a key that he claimed would open any door. With it, provided each move was planned with care, she could work her way by swift, successive stages out of the camp without having

170

to negotiate the electrified barbed wire. But each move would have to be studied, times would have to be worked out in order to evade the guards. She worked on it for weeks, aided readily by one or two others. But the moment the plan was completed and about to be put into operation, she was quite unexpectedly searched and the key was found. It seemed as though somebody might have talked.

She was of course taken before the commandant and punished.

Later, after consultation on the telephone with Ravensbrück, it was decided to send her back there and again the other two girls, for reasons that are difficult to fathom, were sent back with her. The burly women wardresses greeted them again, as they alighted, with a vigorous and vicious use of their whips. The three girls were shoved and pummelled through the door to the ceremony of inspection with which they were already familiar. They were then taken before Commandant Sühren and Violette received, as she had expected, the lash of his condemnation for this second attempt at escape. Punishment followed inevitably. It would be, she realised, more severe than for just a breach of discipline or for failing to accomplish the expected quota of work. She was sentenced to ten strokes with a stick and to solitary confinement for a week in the Bunker or *Zellenbau,* the prison within the camp. Here the meagre food ration was reduced to but one hot meal every three days. The cell, one of sixty-eight in a stout concrete building, was on the ground floor and so had a window, which was of course kept shut. It was more modern and far better equipped than the rest of the camp. There was a lavatory with a tap above it, as at Fresnes, a bed to herself, with a thin straw mattress on hard boards, and a heavy iron door. There was also surprisingly central heating in these cells, which the huts had not; but, adjustable for individual cells, it was used on occasion for punishment, being turned on full in summer and off in winter. Odette Churchill (now Mrs Hallowes) was at that time in one of the underground cells here and recalls hearing Violette's voice quite clearly one afternoon, talking to one of the guards stationed outside. Violette said: "How do you like

171

being on duty on a Sunday? It should be your day off, or don't you get one?" The man laughed. He said he didn't mind. "Have you to do much more of it? When do you go off?" – "Oh, another hour," he replied. It seems to suggest that even here her mind was exploring the possibilities of escape, through the co-operation possibly of one of the guards. In the cells around were a number of male prisoners. The former Mayor of Vienna was here and alongside him was a professor from one of the German universities with his wife. They were special prisoners. Their cells were well furnished and their rations were more plentiful. They had been brought here, to this camp for women, in order that there should be no trace of them. It was a convenient way of getting them lost.

At the end of the week Violette was taken again before Sühren, who bellowed fresh dire threats. As always she was scornful, for she has been set down as a difficult prisoner – intractable and quite ungovernable.

Flaming with rage, he had her taken away. She was physically fit still, despite the undernourishment and ill-treatment; and, since the shortage of labour was acute, after some days he assigned her to the harsh and strenuous task of laying out a new airfield at Königsberg, not far from the Russian front, where the retreating German armies were in ever-increasing need of bomber-fighter support. Once again the two English girls who had returned with her from Torgau were made to accompany her.

Königsberg stands on the River Oder at what was then the north-eastern corner of Germany. It is more than 300 miles from Ravensbrück and the journey, which was again made by truck, was a long one through pine-clad country. Violette, together with Lillian Rolfe and Denise Bloch, was made to fell trees and then to clear the ground and level it. Arriving there in the first week of November, they found the weather intensely cold and severe. Winter had already set in. They were lodged in an unheated hut. Their clothes were still what they had worn through the summer. The food was no better and their hard labour had to be sustained despite the ceaseless gnawing of their hunger.

Here, as at Torgau, they were not in a concentration camp, but members of a work-party. Most of the others were men, chiefly Russian and Polish prisoners of war, with a sprinkling of French prisoners among them. The small teams of women were required to undertake the same arduous, back-breaking tasks as the men, and SS guards, using whips, saw that their efforts should be unflagging.

During the three months she was here, the three hardest and bitterest months of a bleak Russian winter, Violette suffered the greatest privations. Often for her insubordination and her attitude of contempt she was beaten and denied her scant rations. Her intention unceasingly was to seek the first chance of escape. But, out in the open though they were all day long, it was by no means easy. Police dogs prowled around them. There were guards with loaded rifles on the watch. Wires encircled the encampment. And if, despite these, she succeeded in breaking away, she would have to embark on a long and difficult journey across the tell-tale snow, into Russia perhaps, or back across Germany to the westward. None the less she was resolved to attempt it.

During December the Allied Armies in the West entered Holland and penetrated into Germany at Karlsruhe. In the East the Russians were sweeping through the Baltic States and in January crossed the German frontier into the great industrial regions of Upper Silesia. To the north, much nearer to Königsberg, they crossed the Vistula on both sides of Warsaw. On January 17th they entered Warsaw.

These mighty sweeps from both sides, destined before long to meet in the very heart of Germany, were the subject of many rumours among the prisoners at Königsberg. Excitement was high at the realisation that their liberation must now be near. A sweep northward from Warsaw soon endangered Königsberg itself, and, though the town was heavily defended, it was obvious that it would before long be completely isolated. Violette's hopes now took a fresh turn. She had often wondered, at Ravensbrück and Torgau, which of the Allies would be responsible for her liberation. It seemed clear now that Königsberg would be the prize of the Russians. That would involve, she foresaw, a journey eastward, possibly right across Russia and the steppes of Siberia into China, which happily was on the side of the Allies. Or, more swiftly perhaps, southward to Odessa and through the Black Sea into the Mediterranean. At any rate freedom was now in sight.

But quite suddenly at the end of January Violette and the two other English girls were sent back to Ravensbrück. Was it to prevent their liberation by the Russians? Or was there something more sinister behind this?

In any case in just over three months the war in Europe was over.

Chapter 20

Waiting for News

When the war ended in Europe Violette's parents realised that her return home was imminent. It could not now be more than a matter of days or possibly weeks. Mrs Bushell, who had kept in the closest touch with Tania, visiting her at Mill Hill often two and three times a week, was able to bring her to London. She had prepared a room for her at Brixton and also got Violette's room ready for her home-coming.

But the weeks passed. The war in Japan ended too, and the summer of 1945 was nearly spent without any news at all from her or of her. She must have written, of that they felt certain; with the war over there was nothing now to stop her. The only message they received was the one she had sent from Torgau, which reached them in January. Since then – nothing. There was no longer either bombing or torpedoes or the confusion of war to send letters astray. And yet, a month after the war had ended, they read in the newspapers of a postwoman in their area burning letters in her grate. 'A Stockwell postwoman,' the papers said. On June 11th the caretaker of a block of flats found hundreds of letters strewn about the floor of a flat. Some of the letters were intact, others were torn up. There were also fragments of charred paper in the grate. Many of these letters, it was said in court, for the postwoman was found guilty of stealing postal orders, were from members of the Forces serving abroad. It was possible that a letter from Violette might have been among them.

Inquiries were made of Colonel Buckmaster and Vera Atkins, but they had themselves been trying to get some news.

Mr Bushell called at the War Office, but no information was available there either. He got in touch with the Red Cross. They at least, with their widespread international branches, should be able to trace her. But there too nothing was known, and after months of seeking nothing was learned. The Bushells went to see the Member of Parliament for Brixton, Colonel Marcus Lipton. He took up the inquiries, pursued them through every available channel, but was unable to elicit any news at all.

Unofficially it was said that Violette had undoubtedly been freed when the Russians reached Ravensbrück in April. With the war still in progress at that time and a large slice of Germany separating the Russians from the Allied lines in the west, Violette would necessarily have to make her way home through Russia. It was believed that she was travelling southward to Odessa. It was a long way round of course and would take time; that was no doubt why she had not got home yet.

Bewildered, anxious, and at times a little fearful, her two parents wandered pathetically through London on their forlorn quest, holding hands to give each other courage and hope. The mother, with her large sad eyes, listened, shaking her puzzled head, while the father, his eyes filling often, was doggedly persistent in his questioning and at times even angry when no one could tell him where he might go to obtain definite news. Months had passed since the ending of the war – and still nobody seemed to know. Couldn't anybody do anything? With some difficulty they traced Staunton and wrote to him in North Africa, but he had no news and was too far away to help: he died not long afterwards quite suddenly at his desk at Casablanca. They went again to the War Office and to the Red Cross, to Colonel Buckmaster and to Vera Atkins. Vera, anxious to locate Violette as well as others who were missing, was about to go to Europe herself in their quest. She was resolved to find out. The news would have to be obtained.

Sadly Mr and Mrs Bushell returned to their home. From time to time they wept and went over their memories of her childhood, tender moments, fiery, defiant moments, lighthearted and gay moments that had filled their days with laughter. And after a while they set out still again – to the War Office, to the Red Cross, to the headquarters of the French Section of SOE. Again they wrote letters to their MP and to the Prime Minister. They wrote also to the newspapers and followed up their letters by calling on the editors.

The Press took it up. PARACHUTE GIRL MISSING said the headlines in the latter weeks of 1945 and shortly afterwards one of the newspapers published an interview with three Englishwomen who had been at Ravensbrück and had only just arrived in Sweden. This gave Mr and Mrs Bushell great hope. Violette must be on her way home too and would no doubt be found before long by some newspaper correspondent in China or India.

One of the women who had arrived in Sweden, Mrs Doreen Verani, of Southport, said she had seen three English girls, including one named Corinne. It was, of course, the name by which Violette was known. "She was small and slim, with dark blue eyes. I don't remember the names of the others. All three were parachutists and had demanded to be treated as officers and war prisoners." She had met them, she said, in September 1944, which would have been shortly after their arrival at Ravensbrück from Fresnes. "They were in the camp for a short time before being transported to work in factories or on the roads."

In March 1946, after ten months of persistent seeking since the end of the war, the Bushells received the following reply from the Red Cross office in Geneva:

Comité International de la Croix-Rouge, Agence Centrale des Prisonniers de Guerre, Palais du Conseil-General, Genève. Charles G. Bushell, Esq., 18 Burnley Road, Stockwell, London, S.W.9.

March 29th, 1946.

Dear Sir – We beg to acknowledge receipt of your letter dated 18th inst., concerning:

Violette *SZABO*, taken prisoner in June 1944.

We regret very much to say that we cannot give you any information on your daughter, but, as the inquiries have been taken up by the British Authorities themselves since the cessation of hostilities, we have sent your lines together with the newspaper cutting, to the British Red Cross in London and they shall answer you direct.

Hoping that you shall soon have some news, we beg to remain ...

That same month some of the newspapers, approached again by the Bushells, published a picture of little Tania, now aged three and a half. She was shown gazing at a photograph of her mother. Under it were these words: 'Wondering, she gazes at a picture of her missing mother'. Her imprisonment at Ravensbrück was then referred to and the caption added: 'Since then nothing has been heard of her, and the War Office thinks the chances of her being still alive are "extremely remote". But her parents, Mr and Mrs C.G. Bushell, of Burnley Road, Stockwell, SW, refuse to give up hope'.

Among those who saw this picture was Mrs Julie Barry, living at Nettlebed in Oxfordshire. She told the *News of the World* that she was in Guernsey when the Germans came and that she had been taken to Germany as a prisoner.

"At Ravensbrück," she said, "I was made a prison policewoman and given the number 39785 and a red band with letters on it to indicate my status.

"I was handed a heavy leather belt with instructions to beat the other women prisoners. It was a hateful task, but in it I saw my only chance to help some of the condemned women."

She claimed to be the last person to see Violette alive, the last person to speak to her.

"It was this camp into which three British parachutists were brought. One was Violette Szabo. They were in rags, their faces black with dirt, and their hair matted. They were starving. They had been tortured in attempts to wrest from them secrets of the invasion, but I am certain they gave nothing away.

"Mrs Szabo told me all about herself – about her dead

soldier husband and her child, to whom she was devoted. I think that she and her two companions knew they had been brought to Ravensbrück to die. Even among the thousands of women in the camp these three were outstanding. They were British and the Germans knew it. Nothing could break their spirit.

"One morning came the order for the three of them to go to the Commandant's office. Mrs Szabo walked unaided. The other two were carried. Many of the inmates wanted to die, but Mrs Szabo and her companions wanted to live to tell the world how they had been treated."

The War Office immediately sent two men to interview Mrs Barry. Mrs Bushell was later asked if she would care to see the woman herself, but she flatly refused to speak to anyone who had been a camp policewoman at Ravensbrück.

Was this statement of hers correct? Mr and Mrs Bushell could not believe that their daughter was dead.

Vera Atkins meanwhile had set out on her personal search for news of those secret agents who were still missing. In the course of her wanderings in Europe she visited the jail at Minden where many who had been in positions of authority at Ravensbrück were awaiting their trial. On April 13th, 1946, she saw Johann Schwarzhuber, the camp Führer. He had been second in command at Ravensbrück, but the Commandant Fritz Sühren had anticipated the coming of the Russians by taking Odette Churchill across to the Allied lines in the hope that he might obtain his own freedom in exchange for her deliverance. He was, however, arrested, but managed to escape.

Schwarzhuber had been interrogated since his arrest, but so far had declined to say anything except that he was not personally responsible for what had happened. He had been acting under orders from his superiors, he said, and quite often his subordinates had acted on their own initiative.

Vera Atkins, after a prolonged attempt at trying to make the man speak, said: "I am greatly concerned about three girls who were in your camp at Ravensbrück. But you are running true to type, Schwarzhuber. Once you were pleased to have your rank and the responsibility it conferred. Today you deny all knowledge of what was done. It amazes me that you should do so.

"I shall leave you now, but in a few hours I shall be back. I want you to think about it, Schwarzhuber. I am not saying 'Try to remember'. You remember all right. You could not possibly forget. I am asking you to think about what I have said."

As she turned to go, he lowered his eyes. He was a dark, squat man, with tired eyes behind his pince-nez.

"All right," he said. "I'll tell you." He thereupon made a statement. It was brief. He said:

I declare that I remember that I had delivered to me towards the end of January 1945, an order from the German Secret Police countersigned by the Camp Commandant Sühren, instructing me to ascertain the location of the following persons – Lillian Rolfe, Danielle Williams [Williams was her code name; her real name was Bloch], Violette Szabo. These were at that time in the dependent camp of Königsberg on the Oder and were recalled by me. When they returned to the Camp they were placed in the punishment block and moved from there into the block of cells.

One evening, towards 1900 hours, they were called out and taken to the cemetery yard by the crematorium. Camp Commandant Sühren made these arrangements. He read out the order for their shooting in the presence of the Chief Camp Doctor, Dr Trommer, SS Sergeant Zappe, SS Lance-Corporal Schult or Schulee [a block leader from the men's camp], SS Corporal Schenk [in command of the crematorium], Dentist Dr Hellinger. I was myself present.

The shooting was done by Schult with a small-calibre gun through the back of the neck. They were brought forward singly by Corporal Schenk. Death was certified by Dr Trommer. The corpses were removed singly by internees who were employed in the crematorium and burnt. The clothes were burnt with the bodies.

I accompanied the three women to the crematorium yard. A female camp overseer was also present and was sent back when we reached the crematorium. Zappe stood guard over them while they were waiting to be shot.

All three were very brave and I was deeply moved. Sühren was also impressed by the bearing of these women. He was annoyed that the Gestapo did not themselves carry out these shootings.

I recognise with certainty the photograph of Danielle Williams and I think I recognise the photograph of Lillian Rolfe. I know that the third had the name of Violette.

I am prepared to make this declaration under oath. Read, found correct and signed of my own free will.

Vera Atkins took it down in German. "You realise," she said, "that this is deeply incriminating."

He said he did. She then signed it too and it was entered as his deposition at the trial.

It will be noticed in this statement that there were some officials as well as some internees and at least one other attendant present. That there was talk of it afterwards in the camp is clear from what Mrs Julie Barry said in the interview published in the newspapers. Schwarzhuber told Vera Atkins in the course of a short talk afterwards that Lillian Rolfe was ill and could not walk. She was suffering apparently from lung trouble and had to be assisted to the place of execution. A sketch showing a part of the camp, the block of cells where the three girls were confined and their place of execution, was made by Vera Atkins with the guidance of Schwarzhuber. It shows that quite a long walk was necessary. They had to go from the cells through the camp, past the kitchen and the wash-room, up to the massive gate leading out of the camp; then on the outer side of the walls a correspondingly long walk had to be undertaken all the way down again to a point opposite the cells in the Bunker. Here, on a grass patch adjoining the crematorium, the girls were executed. Mrs Julie Barry persists that two of the girls had to be carried on stretchers and only Violette was able to walk. "On each face," she adds, "was a look of contempt for the guards."

Violette, they say, was the last to be executed and had to suffer the agony of seeing her friends put to death, aware all the time that the same fate awaited her. She did not flinch. Her spirit was indomitable. Again and again in the past, when all seemed lost, she had fought her way out – with her wits at Rouen, with a gun, despite overwhelming odds, at Salon-la-Tour, where she rose again after her injury and fought even when they came to seize her. Even in captivity she tried repeatedly to break away so that, returning, she could fight on. But now there seemed to be no way out at all. With such power as still remained to them, the Germans, encircling her here with guards, held her at their mercy. It was her turn now. Lifting her head with haughty scorn, she walked the last few paces to her death.

Schwarzhuber was sentenced to death after his trial at Hamburg and was hanged. Fritz Sühren, a fugitive for some years, was caught eventually, tried and also executed.

Chapter 21

Tania Puts On Her Party Dress

Following Vera Atkins' talk with Schwarzhuber, the War Office, able at last to supply facts, wrote instantly to Mr and Mrs Bushell.

> We have now obtained from an eyewitness news of her fate. This witness was the camp overseer who is now under arrest. Mrs Szabo, together with two friends, was executed by shooting one evening by special command of the German Secret Police. The witness has testified that the bearing of the three women was of the highest order and greatly impressed all those that performed or who were present at the execution. Death was instantaneous and the body was immediately cremated.
>
> In giving this news to you, news which I know must be very difficult to bear, I should like to offer on behalf of this Branch my own very sincere sympathies. You must be very proud of the way your daughter maintained her calm dignified courage throughout her ordeal. It is testimony of that courage that she impressed and moved even those responsible for her death.

The news was of course shattering, coming as it did after months of hope, however slender it may often have seemed. They were appalled by the cold-blooded and barbaric manner of her execution and the complete senselessness of it all. Without any pretence at a trial, she had been brought back all the way from Königsberg to Ravensbrück and killed just as the war was about to end, when she was no longer in a position to endanger any plans of the German High Command. Why, they asked themselves again and again, why this deliberate and quite brutal murder? Why were these three English girls singled out for execution from among the thousands of other prisoners in the camp? An intense hate had been fostered by the German hierarchy against the British throughout the long years of war, born no doubt of the realisation that only British stubbornness had denied them their triumph and caused their country to be now in ruins. In part this was responsible for the British prisoners being treated far more harshly than the rest. But not all the British women in Ravensbrück, although a mere handful, were executed. The ones singled out to die were those who had been made to suffer the most atrocious tortures, and that apparently was what the Germans wanted to cover up. Their aim was to obliterate the evidence that these women would be able to give of their vile and brutal behaviour. If they were allowed to live, much would be revealed and many in authority now would undoubtedly be called to account by the victors. Thus, when the tide turned, the order went forth and to it was attached a list of names. The list was scrutinised carefully. The location of those on it had to be ascertained, as Schwarzhuber revealed in his statement. Odette was spared because it was felt that the name of Churchill might be of some value at the eventual reckoning.

And so, during the days and nights of darkness she had to endure in the Bunker – in an underground cell now which was kept in total darkness so that when the light was suddenly switched on, as an eye was applied to the peep-hole, it was quite blinding – Violette must have known that the end was very near. She heard the firing squads at their fell work only a few yards from where she lay, and she breathed in the suffocating smoke from the crematorium on the other side of the wall. Often she heard screams when the crematorium doors were opened, which suggests that some at least of those thrust into it were still alive, despite the assurance given by Schwarzhuber to the court about a doctor examining the bodies after execution.

With the passage of time the parental hurt was assuaged a little and their hearts were filled with a great pride at the courage and the vast capacity of endurance of their daughter. The adventurous-ness of her spirit in childhood, her unshakeable will, her moments of defiance were illumined now with a new light.

From Colonel Buckmaster, chief of the French Section of SOE, they received a warm personal letter, in the course of which he said:

> I felt I must write to you at this time, now that more has been learned of Violette's heroic behaviour, to tell you how much we all admired her and how magnificently she upheld the tradition of the French Section, of which we were all very proud.
>
> There are just two facts about Violette's work which you, maybe, do not yet know. The first was her courageous defence of her Headquarters. We know that she fought the Gestapo, armed only with a Sten gun.... She went on firing until she was exhausted.
>
> The second incident was in the train which took her, and a large number of other prisoners of both sexes, to Germany. Between Compiegne and Saarbrücken, the RAF bombed and machine-gunned the train. The German guards, in panic, locked the prisoners in and took shelter. Violette managed to get into the corridor of the train, and, together with another girl, took water to the men who were in another carriage at the far end of the train.
>
> This valiant action greatly cheered the prisoners. We were very proud that Violette took this gallant initiative: British prestige was even further enhanced by her action.
>
> I hope these two incidents will help you to regard with great and legitimate pride the magnificent record of your daughter, who was very dear also to us.

Later that year came the posthumous award of honours. On December 17th, 1946, Violette was gazetted for the George Cross – the first British woman ever to receive it. The citation, though written eighteen months after the war had ended, was based apparently on information officially available in London at the time. There is no mention in it of the ambush at Salon-la-Tour and the chase of close on two miles across the countryside, but it refers instead to a house in which she and 'other members (plural) of her group' were surrounded by the Gestapo. The citation states:

> Madame Szabo volunteered to undertake a particularly dangerous mission in France. She was parachuted into France in April 1944, and undertook the task with enthusiasm. In her execution of the delicate researches entailed she showed great presence of mind and astuteness She was twice arrested by the German security authorities, but each time managed to get away. Eventually, however, with other members of her group, she was surrounded by the Gestapo in a house in the south-west of France. Resistance appeared hopeless, but Madame Szabo, seizing a Sten gun and as much ammunition as she could carry, barricaded herself in part of the house, and, exchanging shot for shot with the enemy, killed or wounded several of them. By constant movement she avoided being cornered and fought until she dropped exhausted. She was arrested and had to undergo solitary confinement. She was then continuously and atrociously tortured, but never by word or deed gave away any of her acquaintances, or told the enemy anything of value. She was ultimately executed. Madame Szabo gave a magnificent example of courage and steadfastness.

It is by no means unusual for an official citation to need revising in the light of subsequent information. There have indeed been instances when, the fresh facts warranting it, a higher award has been made in place of the one conferred earlier. In the case of Violette Szabo it is felt by those who have examined the new evidence that, in view of the fact that there are many witnesses still alive who saw her heroic battle against the swarming hordes of the Das Reich SS Panzer division at Salon-la-Tour, and also because of her act of mercy to the

186

prisoners in the railway train conveying them to Germany when, under fire, she brought water again and again, manacled though she was, to the suffering prisoners, she ought to be awarded the Victoria Cross. Dame Irene Ward, MP, has been persistently advocating that this award should be made.

The *Croix de Guerre* was awarded posthumously by the French Government early in 1947.

On January 28th, 1947, Mr and Mrs Bushell and Violette's daughter were invited to Buckingham Palace to receive the George Cross from the King. For days beforehand Tania, who was four and a half and too young to understand what had happened to her mother, applied herself strenuously to learning how to curtsy – 'skirty' she called it. The pretty French frock which her mother had bought for her at the Trois Quartiers in Paris during her first mission was brought out and ironed with immense pride by Mrs Bushell on the kitchen table, while Tania watched, her chin resting on the edge of the table, her eyes wide with wonder. She was about to wear it at her first party.

The King seemed to know every detail of Violette's great heroism. He told her parents about incidents of which they had not yet heard. He then handed the George Cross to Tania. "It is for your mother. Take great care of it," he said.

Turning to Mr and Mrs Bushell he added: "I don't think I would have had the courage to do what your wonderful daughter did. She really had remarkably great courage."

As they emerged from the palace, photographers surrounded little Tania and asked her to show them the George Cross. She opened the box. The cameras clicked. One of the photographers said: "How wonderful! What a great honour."

"It's for Mummy," said Tania. "I'll keep it for her till she comes home."